To Cher

MW00775279

SURVIVING IN THE SECURITY ALARM BUSINESS

Best Wishes, & Success

Ken Sgimla

SURVIVING IN THE SECURITY ALARM BUSINESS

Lou Sepulveda C.P.P.

BUTTERWORTH
HEINEMANN

Boston, Oxford, Johannesburg, Melbourne, New Delhi, Singapore

Recognizing the importance of preserving what has been written, Butterworth-Heinemann prints its books on acid-free paper whenever possible.

Butterworth–Heinemann supports the efforts of American Forests and the Global ReLeaf program in its campaign for the betterment of trees, forests, and our environment.

Library of Congress Cataloging-in-Publication Data

Sepulveda, Lou.
    Surviving in the security alarm business / by Lou Sepulveda.
      p. cm.
    ISBN 0-7506-7098-3 (alk. paper)
    1. Security systems industry—Management.   2. Burglar alarm industry—Management.   3. New business enterprises—Management.
I. Title.
HD9999.S452S46   1999   98-8176
621.389′28′068—dc21   CIP

British Library Cataloguing-in-Publication Data
A catalogue record for this book is available from the British Library.

The publisher offers special discounts on bulk orders of this book.
For information, please contact:

Manager of Special Sales
Butterworth-Heinemann
225 Wildwood Avenue
Woburn, MA 01801-2041
Tel: 781-960-2500
Fax: 781-960-2620
For information on all Butterworth–Heinemann publications available, contact our World Wide Web home page at: http://www.bh.com

10 9 8 7 6 5 4 3 2 1

Transferred to digital printing 2006

Contents

21

As in the trenches, look at "how to" design, build, develop, motivate, and manage a sales force in today's highly competitive marketplace.

Preface

As I was writing this book, I couldn't shake my desire to have its title reflect the book's "war" theme. I feel strongly that the war metaphor works, and the chapter titles reflect this. Business is war and sales are its battles. We fight for survival, survival of the fittest. However, I believe that, to truly succeed, surviving isn't good enough. *Winning* is my goal. Anything less is just not good enough.

Even companies as big and successful as Microsoft fight a war every day. The firm is a leader, and you can believe its enemies (competitors) are doing everything they can to unseat it, to beat it.

Microsoft employs thousands of people who depend on the company's success for all or part of their livelihood. If Microsoft fails, so does life as they now know it. Thousands more—investors, suppliers, and the like—depend on Microsoft for all or part of their financial existence. Is this war? You bet it is!

The security alarm business is no different. We, too, the companies and the individuals who make up a company, are at war everyday for our financial existence. We fight the battle in the air, with direct mail, radio, and television advertising campaigns designed to soften the marketplace for our troops.

Our navy transports the battalions to the front lines. And, like the army and marines, with our leaders showing the way, our frontline troops—sales, service, and installation—fight the battle on the ground using hand-to-hand combat to win sales over those who would try to beat us.

Unlike the Gulf War, Korean War, or World War II, our soldiers don't physically die in the commission of their duty. However, there are casualties in our war nonetheless.

A salesperson who doesn't sell earns one less commission check. Less money is available to pay the mortgage, rent, tuition, clothing, and of course, food. If the salesperson loses too many sales, a career dies.

When a salesperson doesn't sell, the company's installers have fewer jobs to install. Less income is earned, which the installers need to support themselves and their families.

When a salesperson doesn't sell, one less sales agreement is processed. Enough lost sales means fewer people needed to process paperwork and fewer to monitor and respond to alarms.

Is this a war? You bet it is! In sales and business we fight for the customer's security dollar every day. Nothing happens until a sale is made.

To enjoy success in any business we must understand the war we're in. We must know our enemies (competition) as well or better than they know themselves. We must know their strengths so we may defend ourselves against them. We must know their weaknesses so we can attack them.

We must plan our mission, determine the hills we must take and occupy. We must train our leaders so that they can successfully recruit, train, and motivate our troops to win. We must heal our injured so they may be ready to resume the fight. And, yes, we must bury our dead.

In today's highly competitive arena, companies involved in selling directly to the consumer face a competitive environment unlike anything they've ever faced in the past. Huge companies like ADT, Brinks, Ameritech (a phone company), Entergy, Westar (both very large utilities), and many other major corporations are duking it out for the consumer's security dollar. And, believe it, these companies have the money and know-how to succeed in business.

ADT, the biggest of them all at the time of this writing, is getting bigger every day. In 1989, ADT monitored approximately 450,000 customers in the United States, making it the biggest alarm company at the time. It now has over 2 million monitored customers. Through ADT's branch operations and authorized dealers, the company is growing by over 400,000 new customers each year.

Every day the word on the street announces yet another company acquired by one of the giants. And the field of battle becomes smaller and better defined.

If you are in the security alarm business today, you must ask yourself some very important questions. You must ask yourself in which arena you wish to compete. Will you compete in the highly volatile and competitive high-volume, low-end business, or will you be more of a full-service "niche" provider—offering alarms, stereo, central vacuum, home theater, home automation, and other services.

Are you ready to fight? Are you prepared to win? If you want to know how, then read on.

Introduction—War Planning

Whether your company is an existing company with many years of doing business under its corporate belt or a brand spanking new enterprise, today's competitive business world requires that businesses rethink their corporate mission, analyze their paradigms, and reengineer their corporation in preparation for the 21st century and beyond.

To start the reengineering process, you must first set aside how you have been conducting business and focus your thoughts and plans on how you should do business in the future in response to market changes and trends. Consider today as the first day in business. Knowing what you know now, free of the baggage you carry from your past years in business, how would you re-create your business?

Had the Swiss done this, they would have developed the quartz watch instead of discarding the idea as not fitting their paradigm of how a watch should work. When presented with the quartz watch design, they would have given the product a chance. Instead, they compared this new technology to the way they designed and built watches and concluded a quartz watch did not possess the precision workmanship and quality present in the Swiss-made watch: "This is not how a Swiss watch is made." So they passed on the idea. Not so many years later, the Swiss watch industry is suffering, lagging behind technology it let slip out of its hands. Technology that their paradigms and pride would not let them accept.

Had the railroads stepped outside the paradigm box they built for themselves, they would have recognized the potential for yet another form of transportation developing before their eyes and founded a hugely profitable new division to handle air transportation. Instead, they fell back in their comfortable paradigm, buried their heads in the sand, saying to themselves, this "upstart" will go away. Flying will never replace us. We own the transportation market. We, after all, are the great American railroads. We changed the face of America. And so, as they say, the rest is history.

Then, there is the great American auto industry—the Big Three. No one knew more about building and marketing the automobile better than Ford, General Motors, and Chrysler. The world agreed.

Had they looked beyond the boundaries of their personal and professional paradigms, they would have been open to the suggestions of consultants who approached American business with radical ideas like the "quality circle." Instead, they shooed away those radical-thinking consultants who dared to suggest the Big Three didn't have a corner on brain power in management of automotive manufacturing, forcing the consultants to go to Japan to incubate their ideas about the future of building automobiles. And, almost before they could say Toyota, cars made in Japan became the car of choice for all too many Americans. Cars made everywhere but the United States became the high-quality choice for the American consumer.

So climb out of your personal paradigm and think like the entrepreneur you are. Ask yourself the following questions:

1. What is the best way to market my products and services?
2. Who is a prospect and why? Has this person or company changed or is in the process of changing?
3. How should I take products to market?
4. Based on some of these conclusions, what should my growth goals be for the next 12 months?
5. Will I, or should I, continue to sell products at the price point at which I presently sell them?
6. Should I venture into the high-volume, low-price end of the market?
7. Looking at my product as units instead of pieces or parts, how many units should I plan for?
8. At what pace should I grow my business?
9. If I chose to grow my business, how will I fund that growth?
10. Looking forward 20 years, where is this industry going? How can I prepare my company so that it remains a viable organization for myself or my heirs?

Pick Your Battlefield

THE SECURITY ALARM BUSINESS

For the first hundred years or so of the security alarm business, alarm companies of every kind focused only on "high-end" dollar selling. The goal was to make a profit at the point of sale. There was nothing else to "fall back on."

In the early 1970s, when I first ventured into the alarm business, which, at the time, was primarily a fire alarm sales business, the average price of an alarm system was easily in the range of $1000 and up. Monitoring was a feature seldom sold— and for good reason. Digital dialers were just being invented, so the only way to monitor an alarm system was by way of direct wire and McCullough loop circuits. These products required monitoring stations equipped with hundreds of telephone lines dedicated to the monitors. Starting a monitoring center was extremely costly. The wholesale monitoring services readily available today had not yet started. In addition, alarm buyers were primarily businesses, especially large businesses or those dealing in expensive inventory (banks, jewelry stores, furriers), and the very wealthy homeowner. All these factors made the sale of alarm services a poor choice for the small to medium-size business. These firms just couldn't compete.

In the 1980s, combination burglar and fire alarm systems commonly were sold and the average price for the package system sold throughout the country climbed to over $2000. Monitoring became the primary reason alarm companies claimed to be in business. Sure, some companies sold systems for $600–800, but they were few and far between, and most, we were certain, would go out of business within a year. However, many didn't, and the beginning of a major change in the security alarm industry had begun.

I vividly remember two such startup companies I competed with in the early to late 1970s. The first, Guardian Security Systems, started by Charlie Yuspeh, quickly became a thorn in my side. While the average cost of an alarm system we sold to a very demanding, wealthy, uptown client went for $1500, Charlie sold his for an average of $850. Making matters worse, Charlie was a respected and well-known member of the community. Needless to say, Charlie's company presented us with tough competition. However, we were sure he'd soon go out of business. After all, we thought, he wasn't charging near enough for his services. Charlie did not go out of business.

Worse than Charlie was the next big competitor to challenge the way things were done: Electronic Security Systems, also known as ESS. Before entering the alarm business, the owners of ESS, a couple of brothers, sold door to door a variety of products, from vacuum cleaners to cemetery plots. Now they were selling alarm systems. And worse, they had the audacity to "peddle" alarm systems as they did vacuums, door to door. Didn't they know this couldn't be done, we thought? Didn't they realize door-to-door selling in the alarm business was unprofessional?

The local alarm community was aghast by what was going on. And, of course, to make matters worse, ESS sold their products for easily half the price charged by the top local companies.

To many of us so-called security professionals, everything about ESS spelled *junk*. We laughed about it. No way could they survive! In fact, when the ESS president applied to join the local chapter of the NBFAA (National Burglar and Fire Alarm Association), the membership blackballed him. No way were we going to allow this company to say it was one of us.

Today, over 22 years later, ESS is still in business and probably is the biggest and most successful locally owned company in its region of the country. ESS was ahead of the paradigm shift.

Like all companies who dare to go against conventional wisdom, ESS was looked upon as a troublemaker, a startup that must be put in its place. The company is doomed to fail; and good riddance, we all agreed.

The owners of ESS had a couple of advantages, one of which we, the local alarm industry, gave them. First, they didn't know better. They didn't know the paradigm they were supposed to be controlled by. They left one business for another and simply did what they knew how to do. Sell and make a profit.

Second, we didn't let them join our club. We didn't let them join the local association, where they might have been infected by our beliefs and paradigms. We did them a huge favor and didn't realize it.

ESS was probably five years or so ahead of the paradigm shift.

You've probably read about paradigm shifts, and if you are old enough, you have witnessed the more obvious paradigm shifts of the past 40 years, such as when "Made in Japan" no longer meant junk but high quality and when automobiles built in the United States came to mean unreliable instead of the best. However, we may not have noticed the paradigm shift that occurred in the security alarm business.

As I look back, the first paradigm shift affecting the security alarm industry occurred when the emphasis on alarm monitoring overtook the emphasis on selling and making a profit on the installation. Before monitoring, in the early 1970s, alarm companies had to rely on point of sale profit, like most other businesses today, without the benefit of recurring revenue.

Sometime in the mid-1980s the shift occurred, and the emphasis changed to building monitoring revenue. Security alarm professionals all over the country argued that the only reason they were in business was to drive recurring revenue. They made a case that the sale of the alarm product was just a means to that end. As that belief grew, prices fell. The emphasis on adding accounts to the recurring revenue base at all cost replaced the goal to make an immediate, one-time profit. In the late 1990s and into the 21st century, we will witness yet another shift—back to the way the industry thought in the 1970s.

As the price point of alarm systems continue to plummet; and as the "giants" (ADT and Brinks) drive the market; and as the R Box, Ameritech, and large electric and gas utilities (such as Entergy and Western Resources) enter the field of play, a new way to do business is emerging. Unless you have deep pockets, competing in the low-end alarm business can be financially devastating. That is, unless you shake off the paradigm you're living in and look at the possibilities through new eyes.

Businesses of all kinds stay alive by selling a product at a profit. They prosper without recurring revenue. Good old-fashioned customer service and word of mouth advertising combined with sales ability and entrepreneurship grows their business, generating more profit. Recurring revenue to them means the customer coming back for more or the customer referring friends to buy.

So, before you take the next step toward the 21st century, ask yourself if the paradigm has shifted. Ask yourself how you intend to meet the challenges ahead. How will you compete in this highly volatile marketplace? Will you seek a way to compete with the "big guys" in the high-volume, low-price arena? Or are you going to focus on custom high-end work? You can't do both effectively. Weigh the facts and make the decision. Then plan your attack over the next year and subsequently the next five years.

Are you ready to start? Then, shake off your present paradigms. Rethink your mission, and begin the process toward the future.

2

The Battle Plan

Company owners who attend my seminars often ask me how they can plan for the next five years when they're not sure what will happen next week? If you've not had a lot of experience doing annual forecasts and budgets, the feeling is completely understandable. My answer is to start your plan with a WAG (wild assed guess).

If you have never produced a formalized business plan that spans a number of years, it may seem hard to do. However, if you take a look back at your financial records for last year or, if you are new, look forward and think of the possibilities, you can begin a WAG plan. As the months click off and you check your present results against the plan, an EWAG (educated wild assed guess) will emerge.

INSPECT WHAT YOU EXPECT

Once you have a plan, it is important you inspect your results to the plan monthly. Constant tweaking and evaluation of the plan will produce a living document or plan that can carry you into

11

the next century. But don't bury your head in the sand in the process. Look around yourself from time to time. Ask yourself if things are changing that can dramatically affect your plan. Maybe it's time to discard the plan and start anew. Maybe another paradigm shift is under way.

Create a projected profit and loss statement that concurs with your growth plan. Determine if your goals are consistent with your ability to raise capital. Growing too fast without available capital has put more than one well-intentioned entrepreneur into bankruptcy court. Many "successful" entrepreneurs are in bankruptcy court today, asking themselves how they got there. Their companies actually have succeeded themselves to death.

If the conclusion of your future thinking suggests you grow the business, which means adding to your sales staff and subsequently to the support staff necessary to handle growth, you'll need to ask yourself some important planning questions.

WHO, WHAT, WHEN, AND HOW?

Ask yourself who is going to do what when.

Who?

Who is going to determine how to locate the personnel needed to grow the business?

Finding the right people in any organization is critical to its success. How to find them is a constant challenge. If you are using the newspaper classifieds to locate employees, a lot of thought must be put into the style and content of the ads you place. Consider the possible competition your ad is up against. How attractive and appealing your ad is will dictate how many candidates will respond and whether the right candidate even sees the ad.

As an exercise, look through this Sunday's classifieds. Look through it as if you were looking for a job. The first thing you'll notice is that it is painful to read all the ads. You just won't do it. Even people who badly need a job find it difficult to read every single advertisement without skimming.

So, as you look through the paper this Sunday, pay special attention to what grabs your attention as you read. Some ads will reach up and grab you. Others are so badly done or so busy, you just can't force yourself to read them.

Cut out the ads that grab your attention. Circle or underline the key phrases that excite you and make notes to avoid using the phrases or ads that turn you off or appear unbelievable. As you peruse the classifieds, you'll find ads that are beyond belief, such as *Earn $150,000 per year in your spare time.*

The value of this exercise is that you will learn from master ad writers about what works and what doesn't.

Build a file of ads and key phrases you like. When it comes time to run the ad, you'll be ready. Think back to when you last looked through the employment ads in search of a job.

When should you run the newspaper ad and how should you run it? Should the ad be run for a weekend or a week? Should it be in-column or display?

My experience has proven weekends best. I prefer to run an ad on Sunday only or, at most, Saturday, Sunday, and Monday. When I have surveyed respondents in the past as to when they read the want ad I ran, the majority indicated reading the Sunday ads only.

The decision between in-column versus display ads depends largely on your individual market and the type person you're looking for. If you are looking for a salesperson who has outside sales experience and is in the income range of about $50K per year and up, look at your Sunday paper and determine if the display ads are advertising for that type salesperson. If not, then an in-column ad is all you need.

When your ad runs, cut out the page your ad appears on in the newspaper. Add a cover sheet indicating some important facts about the day the ad appeared. What was the weather like? Did anything special happen that day that would or could distract applicants. What was the placement like? Was your ad way in the back of the section where you placed it? Did the ads on either side of your ad distract from your ad?

Having made notes about the ad, file it until after that particular hiring is over, then make notes on how well the ad pulled. How many applicants answered the ad? What quality were the applicants? Ask the applicants what about the ad interested them. Then file the ad away for future reference.

After doing this a few times, you'll develop a reference library of ads, making the chore of finding good sales candidates much easier.

If you choose to use a blind ad, place more than one small ad in the paper on the same day. They'll likely appear in different columns. This way you have a better chance of a candidate seeing it. It's like being in a raffle with more than one ticket.

What?

Which methods of recruiting will I use? Other than the classified section of your local newspaper, there are a number of other ways to locate people.

Employment agencies supply many people to the workforce. However, other than for management positions, I haven't found them to be very effective. Cost is another consideration. Hiring salespeople is expensive enough without the additional cost of an employment agency fee.

Universities are an excellent source of salespeople. In today's competitive society, graduates from a university are having a difficult time finding decent employment. Go to the universities and meet with the career or guidance counselors. Tell them about the career available to their students with your organization. A career in the sales business is honorable and well paid. Ask permission to set up a display on career day on campus.

Do you have a portable display you use for trade shows? Use it for career day at your local universities. Be prepared to demonstrate the income potential and career opportunities available to bright people. Think about the career opportunities your company has for talented people. What if you hired three very talented individuals this year, what would that do for your production? Would you consider duplicating the process in another city or on the other side of town? Doesn't that mean you'll be in the market for good, experienced management? I think so. So tell the bright people you meet on career days about the ground floor opportunity your company has for a hardworking, bright, and talented person.

Be prepared to overcome the negative programming that some universities are guilty of implanting in their students. An associate of mine recently recounted a conversation he had with a good friend and fellow graduate of the university he attended. He graduated with a degree in education. After graduation, since good teaching jobs didn't materialize immediately, he took a sales job with a medical equipment company, thinking he'd quit to take a teaching position as soon as one became available.

Over a period of time, he found he was succeeding in the sales field. He realized that, not only was he enjoying sales, he was making far more money than he would have or could have as a teacher. When he thought back to the negative programming he received from his college professors, which basically said that if you can't get a real job with a good company, you could probably start in sales until you are able to transfer into a real position, such as accounting or engineering, he grew angry. In other words, sales is the last thing you should want to do. Only if all else fails. Only if you're a failure. After being programmed in this manner, it's no wonder most college grads aren't actively pursuing a career in sales.

As a career, sales is one of the most lucrative, personally rewarding, and satisfying jobs one can have. However, as a rule, sales is not a career of choice for all too many in sales, rather a career settled with—until something else comes along, something better.

Sales also is a career without universal education structure. Think of almost any other career choice and you can find a structured course of education in that field, available at a university, junior college, or at the very least, a trade school. Not so with sales.

You can obtain a degree in marketing; however, that's not sales. Some companies whose product relies on good selling techniques may develop a short course on selling. But nowhere can you find an institute of higher learning that offers a course on sales.

Why is that so? What's wrong with sales? No one denies the income potential in sales is high. It is no surprise to anyone to learn that the person who moved into the very expensive home in the nicest neighborhood is in sales. Then, why doesn't the university system, or any system of higher learning, offer a course of study in sales?

Perhaps, the reasons are rooted in popular opinion and attitude. I'm reminded of the "thumbnail sketch of life insurance salespeople" described in one university-level psychology textbook. The salesperson

- Didn't choose the occupation but stumbled into it.
- Is ambitious; desires success, money, luxuries.
- Likes selling and business.
- Dislikes aesthetic and scientific activities.
- Is aggressively hostile, sociable on a large scale.
- Depends on others for advice and companionship.
- Is conservative and authoritarian.
- Is sensitive to criticism.
- Is a doer rather than a thinker.
- May exploit others financially.

Two psychologists selling sales selection tests to industry characterized the desirable candidate for a sales career in their promotion literature with these words:

> friendly and outgoing, but when you know him he is arrogant, conceited and not very interested in people ... but when he begins to talk he can be a most persuasive, charming, convincing individual. ... he gains your confidence and makes you feel like the most important person in the world. ... but don't be fooled, he doesn't really like people ... to him people are just objects to be twisted, shaped and manipulated.[1]

Wow! I'm ashamed. Good thing my mother didn't read this description of my field, sales. She would've been ashamed to tell anyone what her son does for a living. Kind of like I peddled drugs to young, innocent children—or worse.

I wonder if the authors of these descriptions of salespeople ever read the book *The World's Greatest Salesman* by Og Mandino. If they had, they would've come to the conclusion, as did I, that sales, not prostitution, is the oldest profession—the most honorable of professions.

Nothing happens ... until a sale is made. Sales is a profession requiring knowledge, skill, intestinal fortitude, confidence in one's own ability, belief, conviction, and plain old courage.

Salespeople are the pioneers of industry. Salespeople go where others are uncomfortable to find prospects and buyers for their company's product and services. Salespeople venture out every day knowing they will meet resistance and rejection in search of the customer who needs and will benefit from their company's products. And everyone back home in the comfort of

---

[1] George W. Dudley, Shannon L. Goodson with Dr. David Barnett. *Earning What You're Worth: The Psychology of Sales Call Reluctance.* Dallas, TX: Behavioral Sciences Research Press, Inc., 1995, pp 5–6.

the offices and plant depend on the salespeople to bring in the orders that keep the businesses and plants running and families fed.

All this said, if you are in sales, it is incumbent on you to treat your profession as a profession and therefore seek whatever is available in continuing education for sales. Make the investment in yourself.

Become a voracious reader of sales books. Attend as many sales seminars as you can afford and then practice your profession using role playing. Practice, practice, and have the courage to practice some more. Remember, practice makes perfect.

How?

Customer Referrals   Ask your existing customers for referrals. If you mail a newsletter to your existing customers every quarter, take advantage of that opportunity to ask them if they know of someone who could fill the opening you have available.

Your customers already trust your company. They were confident enough in your company to entrust you with their business. They know people. They know people who are unhappy in their positions, are changing careers, or have been unexpectedly laid off because of downsizing. They will be doing you and their friend a favor by referring your company. Plus, just as a referral customer finds it easier to buy from you because they already have a friend with a positive, satisfied relationship with your company, their friend who is looking for an opportunity also feels more comfortable already knowing what your customers think of your company, product, and services. That's important when considering working for a new company.

Employee Referrals   Several companies I know use employee referrals for all positions. Essentially, they pay a finder's fee to the employee referring a person who is hired and stays with the company for six months. Some pay an additional bonus if the employee is still employed after 12 months. Some of your best employees can be found this way.

A secondary benefit in rewarding employees for their referrals is that you cause them to focus on and tell friends and acquaintances positive things about your company. They have to brag about you and your company if they're to convince someone else to seek a career there.

How much you offer employees for referrals depends somewhat on how hard it is to find good people in your market. I know of one sales manager who is happily paying $1000 to anyone referring an employee who can be hired and kept after 90 days. In his market, salespeople are very difficult to come by, as the unemployment rate is very low.

My personal preference is to structure a referral program that rewards employees in two installments. The first payment is made if the employee is a keeper after 90 days. The second equal payment is made if the employee is still with the company at the end of 12 months. There is no question in my mind, a program like this easily is worth $1000 to me: $500 paid at the end of 90 days and the balance paid on completion of one year.

Is it worth it to you? To find out, spend some time considering how much it cost you to find and keep a good salesperson. Consider the cost of planning the ad, placing the ad, the cost of the ad, interview time, loss of some production while all this takes place, training after hiring, and so on. If you put dollars to these factors I believe you'll conclude $1000 is cheap.

Put together a program. Advertise the referral program within your company and make a big deal of the first couple of referral fees paid. Post a copy of the referral check made out to the employee on every bulletin board in your office. Soon others will catch on to the advantage of referring good people to you, and then everyone wins—you, the new employee, and the existing employee.

Networking   When you are looking for talented people, tell everyone you come in contact with of your search for good people. The more people who know you are looking, the better are your chances of finding someone. Tell everyone about the advantages a good salesperson enjoys in your field. What else could a person do in life that pays as well as the sales field does while providing such positive results for the buyer.

If a salesperson calls on your business to sell a product or service, this is the time you definitely want to see him or her. Pay close attention to how salespersons present themselves and their company. Hand them an objection and see how they handle it. If you like what you see and hear, offer the salesperson a job.

Lots of people feel they are in dead-end jobs. Either they are looking for something better or are dissatisfied where they are and haven't found the time or the courage to seek other employment. Some of these people are calling on you to sell their wares. See them, you may find a solution to both of your problems.

I know a company that hired a salesperson who was working at an oil change store. The owner of the company took his car into an oil change store for an oil change. As he pulled in, a young man walked up to him and asked him the standard questions one is asked at oil change stores.

A few minutes later, as he waited in the waiting room, the young man joined him and pointed out that his air filter was dirty and needed changing. When the company owner said he'd wait until the next time to change the filter, the young man pointed out how a clean filter improves fuel efficiency and the overall life of the car. He concluded that the company owner should reconsider and install the air filter. The company owner agreed.

Moments later the young man returned to report on the company owner's PCV valve and other replaceable items. Each time the company owner objected to doing it now, and each time the young man countered with reasons why the company owner should make the investment.

After all the work was done, the company owner asked the young man if he was making all the money he wanted to make. The young man answered, saying he made a decent living. The company owner repeated the question, "But, are you making all you would like to make?" To which the young man replied, "No."

The company owner invited the young man to his office to explain the opportunities with his company. At the end of the next year, the young, former oil change employee was the company owner's top salesperson. He earned over $100K his first full year. More than three times his previous best year's salary.

The moral of this story is to be on the lookout for sharp candidates for your sales jobs. They don't always walk into your office looking for a job. They don't always respond to an ad you're running. Sometimes, like this young oil change employee, you find them working for someone else. Keep your eyes open for potential sales candidates.

Which Screening Method Will I Use When the Applicants Respond to the Recruiting?

Unless you have loads of time on your hands every day, developing an effective applicant screening method is a must. Suppose your ad is well written and you're fortunate enough to develop lots of interest in your job opportunity, do you have the time to meet individually with every single applicant?

When you are looking for talented people, you must take the time to do a couple of very important things. You only have one chance to make a first impression and so does the sales applicant. It is your job to make the salesperson want a position with your company; then the salesperson's job is to make you want him or her.

To make the salesperson want your position, it is important that you enthusiastically tell the applicant about the opportunity, your company, your product, and the earning potential for the right applicant. Can you do a good job of selling your company if you have to repeat the story for 50 applicants? And, do you want to invest your valuable time meeting with the wrong applicant?

I find a good telephone screening enables me to thin out the applicants, disqualifying those applicants that clearly don't qualify. However, I usually don't conduct the prescreening interview myself because I can't be sure I'll be in the office all day. I have other business concerns to take care of that can distract me during the day.

I employed the services of an administrative person to do the first screening. When we placed an ad, we let everyone in our organization know that we were running an ad for a salesperson. Instructions were given to pass any callers asking for Mr. Lewis to the administrative person selected to handle the prescreening interview. We ran the ad using the desk name Mr. Lewis so we would know the caller was a sales applicant, enabling us to promptly transfer the caller to the proper person.

The administrative prescreener asked the applicant a series of questions designed to make him or her talk. We wanted to determine if the salesperson was articulate, enthusiastic, and had a background in outside sales, if that's what we were looking for. A salesperson who sounded good was told to expect a call from Mr. Lewis that evening between 5 and 9 PM and asked for a phone number where he or she could be reached between those hours.

The purpose for this exercise was twofold. First, I had more time to conduct a good phone interview after 5 in the evening. Fewer distractions meant I could focus on the task at hand. Second, I wanted to see if the candidate wanted the job bad enough to wait for my call. A side benefit of the late hour call is one could learn a lot about the applicant after 5 PM. For example, if the applicant had a substance abuse problem, it was likely to show up in the evening.

Who Will Screen the Calls?

Do I have the time, or should I have someone on staff do it? As mentioned already, I employ an administrative person to screen my calls. You should determine if you have the time to do it yourself. Remember, if you are busy and likely to be interrupted during a phone screening, don't do it. If you can't concentrate, you might miss something important.

What Interviewing Method Will I Use—Single Shot or Shotgun?

If you have only a couple of applicants to interview, a single shot process works just fine. In the single shot process, you conduct a standard one-on-one interview, usually lasting approximately a half-hour.

If, however, you have lots of applicants, there is a real advantage to a shotgun interview. In a shotgun interview, you invite everyone in to interview at the same appointment time, let's say 9 AM.

As applicants arrive, they are given an application to complete and a psychological exam designed to determine if they possess the personality traits and behavior style I look for. Once everyone has completed the application and test, I address the group with an apology. I apologize for bringing everyone in together and then explain why it was necessary to do so:

> Because there are so many applicants and because I know everyone wants to know what this opportunity is, what the company is, what the product is, and what the income and benefits are, I felt I could accomplish this task better by telling everyone about what we're offering at one time. If, after hearing about this opportunity, you are interested in pursuing employment with our company, you will get an opportunity to individually interview. If not, you will simply leave. Fair enough?

Seldom did anyone have a problem with this concept. Applicants did want to know about the company, the products sold, the services provided, why anyone would want to own the product, what was expected from salespeople, and of course, how much and how income is earned.

From that point forward, I demonstrated exactly what I expected them to do if I hired them. I told them about the benefits a prospect would enjoy doing business with our company. The same way I would expect them to tell a prospect about our company.

I demonstrated our products and services, explaining the benefits and value of the product. The same way they should if they worked for my company. If they were impressed with what they saw; if they were impressed with the company, product, and services; if they were satisfied there was a real need for the product and service after the presentation, a couple of very important things happened.

First, they were more likely to realize why a prospect might want to buy the product and therefore how they could make a nice living selling the company's products and services. Second, if they were impressed by the quality of the presentation itself, they were more likely to want to learn how to do just such a presentation. This made it easier to introduce a planned presentation in the training class after we hired them.

Therefore, the person who conducts this group presentation must be able to do a professional presentation. The presentation made should be consistent with the presentation format the salespeople will be taught after they're hired.

What Qualities or Experience Am I Looking for in an Applicant?

Deciding which candidates fit your job best can be difficult, especially when you have a lot of candidates to choose from. It helps to list those qualities you like in an employee as well as those qualities your experience tells you will produce the best results. The following list of 21 qualities is what I use.

Personable
Charming
Confident
Warm, smiling
Caring
Empathetic
Makes good eye contact
Good listener
Compassionate
Good speaker
Trustworthy
Professional
Ambitious
Focused
Goal oriented
Competitive
Good dresser
Good grooming habits
Conviction
Integrity
Self-motivated

Outside sales experience is not always necessary in selling. It will take longer to bring the new, inexperienced sales trainee up to speed if you have to teach the fundamentals of selling, too. However, you won't have to untrain bad habits.

There are people who should be salespeople and don't know it. Installers, service technicians, accountants, secretaries, lawyers, and Indian chiefs may have latent sales ability. If you have a full-time sales training staff, you can develop those candidates and enjoy success with them. Just make sure you have the time or resources necessary to pull it off.

I wouldn't have answered the ad for Kirby Vacuums, if it said it was for a sales job. I didn't consider myself a salesperson. Because the ad was vague, I answered it.

I took the job and was successful. If it wasn't for Kirby, I'm not sure I would have ever entered the selling profession, and that would have been a shame. Kirby had a training program and hired salespeople every week. The company would hire three or four people in the beginning of the week and by week's end was lucky if one remained. The process to find a salesperson was akin to finding a needle in a haystack. However, Kirby found them.

If your plan is to concentrate on high-volume, low-end sales, hiring people who have no previous sales experience works well. Package selling requires less salesmanship. Don't get me wrong. I'm not taking anything away from the salespeople in low-end selling. They are professional salespeople. It's just easier to start in sales that way.

Also, to be successful in low-end selling, it is almost mandatory one canvass door to door. Here is where hiring rookies really pays off. Young, ambitious first-time salespeople will more readily follow their leaders into the field to knock on doors. They'll do it with the enthusiasm the job requires and will succeed. Sometimes, it's difficult convincing an "experienced" salesperson to do the same. Sometimes, they think they've paid their dues and shouldn't have to knock on doors. However, the reality is that knocking on doors is the quickest and easiest way to get going and keep going in low-end residential sales.

Articulate A salesperson who can communicate in an intelligent, concise manner can sell. Selling is communicating a series of thoughts and ideas to a prospect. I don't want to hire any candidate who can't speak intelligently. The phone interviews are designed to uncover the sales applicant's ability to speak. Of course, I'll learn more during the rest of the interview process as well as during training after they are hired.

Being able to communicate doesn't mean that a person with an accent cannot succeed. It doesn't mean applicants must be the best speakers around. It means they must have the ability to convey their thoughts in a way the prospect can understand. They must learn to speak with enthusiasm, confidence, and conviction. They must excite you.

Some of the most intelligent people in the world cannot communicate well. And yet I've hired salespeople who lacked a high school diploma but were terrific communicators and terrific salespeople.

Have the screener ask the applicant to describe in detail a time in their life when they accomplished a task they're especially proud of. The task could have been in school, in sports, anything at all. How excited they can get and how well they're able to describe the accomplishment is what I'm looking for. However, if they're young, don't be too surprised if they can't recall anything.

Professional Appearance Just like poor Pig-Pen in the Charlie Brown comic strip, you just can't dress up some people. Remember, the way the applicants look during the interview is the best they will look. Don't think you can clean them up. Their appearance usually goes downhill after the interview.

Of course, an exception should be made for someone who works in construction or a similar field and had to come to the interview straight from the job, but that's the exception. People who make a professional appearance stand a better chance of succeeding in sales.

Applicants who are applying for their first professional job (excluding part-time jobs at the hamburger stand while in high school) may not own a suit. However, I still expect to see them nicely dressed, dressed as they would if they were going to a family member's wedding or to church.

Caring   In the security business, I want to employ salespeople who truly care about the prospect. Usually when a salesperson truly cares, the prospect feels it and is more likely to buy. Also, the prospect is much more likely to recommend a salesperson whom they perceive truly cares about them.

Conviction   A salesperson who possesses conviction is almost unstoppable. The security alarm business is a life safety business. We truly save lives when we protect people with a high-quality burglar and fire alarm system. The salesperson who has strong conviction will soon develop strong beliefs and conviction about the need for my company's product and services. Nothing sells the prospect on the need for a security system better than the conviction exuding from a salesperson who believes everyone needs one.

You most often can create conviction within a salesperson once he or she understands how important your services can be to a prospect. However, some people never really get the point. I've met security professionals with years of experience who don't have or exude conviction. Ask the applicant during the interview to tell you about anything he or she feels strongly about.

Empathy   The ability to empathize is the ability to understand the prospect's feelings. Empathy does not mean you agree with the prospects feelings, rather you understand how they could feel the way they do.

The salesperson who demonstrates empathy, once again, is the salesperson people like to buy from. Prospects like to feel the salesperson understands their feelings and concerns, even if it is their concern about buying any product from a salesperson without taking some time to think over the decision. Because they show empathy, the salesperson more easily will overcome the "think it over" objection.

Honesty and Integrity   The security business, where I spent 28 years hiring and developing strong salespeople, is a business of trust. The prospect has to trust the security professional in order to buy from him or her. The prospect is placing his or her family and possessions in the hands of the salesperson. Trust is everything.

For my peace of mind and for the peace of mind of the prospect, I must be sure the salespeople I hire are trustworthy, honest, and possess a high degree of integrity. If your business enjoys a high percentage of referrals, it is important to your business that your employees—all of them—possess a high degree of honesty and integrity.

3

Finding the Right Soldiers—the Selection Process

If only we had a crystal ball, finding the best salespeople would be easy. Selecting the right person for a sales position is difficult at best. If we could peer into the future to determine which candidates would perform according to plan, developing a great sales organization would be a snap. However, we cannot.

All we have is our ability to sort between fact and fiction in interviews, our (not always reliable) gut instincts, background checks (if we get answers to our inquiries), and a variety of testing instruments designed to tell us more about the person we're interviewing.

Let's start with testing instruments. Any number of personality tests are available on the open market, ranging in price per test from nothing to $450. While I would question the value of a test that is free; on the surface, $450 is a bit rich for me.

However, ask yourself, how much does it cost to hire sales-people? How much does it cost to plan the ads, place the ads, screen the callers, interview the candidates, train the chosen ones, and lose the people who just don't make it? How much do I lose in productivity while members of my staff and I are in-volved in the recruitment process?

It's been estimated that to hire a salesperson, including everything necessary to hire and bring that person to a point of competence over a 90-day period, can cost, at minimum, $10,000. So therefore, for every successful hire, I must earn approximately $10,000 in profit to cover the cost to hire before the new person is profitable to me. And, for every failure, I've lost $10,000. With that in mind, a $450 test to assist me in determining if I'm hiring the right person doesn't sound so bad anymore.

I know of someone who owns and manages an insurance agency. This agency manager admits investing over $800 on a variety of tests before hiring a new salesperson. However, his retention rate for the salespeople he hires is great. New hires will average over 10 years with his firm. So, then, is the $800 he pays worth it? Based on the success he's enjoying, I'd say a definite yes.

The challenges we face when hiring new people are great. Some sales candidates, especially those with lots of sales experi-ence, have become quite good at interviewing. They know what to say to you and how to excite you about them. Can they deliver as well as they interview?—that is the question.

Sometimes we as managers hire people we personally like. The person who looks like us, who acts like us, who dresses somewhat like us, who likes to do the same things we like to do. Of course, this isn't the criteria we should be using for our hiring process; however, we all too often use it, after all we are just human.

This is one reason why I like using tests to aid in the hiring process. The question then becomes, What type of tests? To help answer that question, we must ask ourselves what we expect from the individuals we're attempting to hire? What must they be able to do to succeed? What behaviors must they possess? We must determine if they *can do* what they must do to succeed. And we must determine if they *will do* what they can do.

CAN DO VERSUS WILL DO

Finding people who can do what is necessary to succeed in direct-to-the-consumer outside sales is relatively easy. Almost anyone can walk down the street and knock on door after door—given a decent script of what to say at the door and after watching someone who is successful knocking on doors. After rehearsing the words, success soon follows.

The problem with this is not whether *they can do it*—of course, they can—it is whether *they will do it*. If they won't get out and knock on doors on their own, knowing they'll succeed easier if they do it, can do alone isn't enough. Your salesperson must be willing to do what it takes to be successful.

Finding salespeople who know people in the area where they'll be selling, making it easier to network with friends and relatives, thus making it easier to find prospects to sell to, is easy. Finding salespeople who are *willing to contact* everyone they know, to let them know they are in the sales business and would appreciate any referrals and leads they may pass on, is yet another matter. The bottom line is, I must find salespeople who can do and will do what it takes to succeed.

Please don't kid yourself. If you interview someone who clearly is unwilling to knock on doors and network, don't think you can change the person. You'll fail more often than you'll succeed.

How can we be sure we find people who will do what is necessary? Testing is available that, when used properly, will uncover *contact hesitation*; that is, a person's fear of self-promotion, the fear of initiating contact with prospective purchasers for a variety of reasons.

In an effort to help you understand and identify the types and degree of contact hesitation (the unwillingness to make the sales call) of the candidates you're going to interview, as well as salespeople you've already hired, let's look at sales contact hesitation and how it portrays itself.

The Entrance Exam

4

If you were to give your new and existing sales staff a checkup from the neck up, would each be diagnosed a professional salesperson?

Why do Greg Norman, Tiger Woods, John Daly, and all the other winning golf pros spend hour after hour, before, during, and after tournaments, practicing hitting golf balls with almost every club in their bag, when they are the best the golf game has to offer? Why does every professional football team devote hours every day during and before the football season practicing to play a game most have played for a minimum of 15 to 20 years? Why, when a professional's game isn't completely on, when the scores are not up to the person's potential, do athletes openly and willingly seek help from a training pro? Golfers will practice hitting balls while being videotaped and then play it back with the trainer looking on in hope of finding the problem in their game—and a solution, a fix that will put them back at the top of their sport, get them winning again.

Yet, professional salespeople seldom, if ever, practice their profession—selling, presenting, probing, handling and overcoming objections, and asking for orders. Nor will they admit having a problem and therefore seek help to correct it. Nor will they seek help when their sales are off, falling dangerously below their own personal averages, when deep in their hearts they know their managers are concerned about their sales production, too.

Why don't salespeople seek help? Why don't they return to the sales practice field to work on every aspect of their profession in an effort to find and then fix the problem? God knows their families depend on the selling skills they possess. Their present and future employment also requires their selling skills to remain sharp.

Could the ego of a salesperson be so brittle that to admit, even for a moment, that one's selling skills are not up to par would shatter his or her delicate ego? Or is the problem really more complicated than that?

Throughout my years as a salesperson, sales manager, and sales trainer, I have witnessed the "death of a salesman" played out all too often in real life. I have witnessed once successful salespeople wither and die on the vine, careers washed up on a psychological reef, nevermore to close the sales they were once capable of producing.

Like other sales managers and trainers I attempted to find the ailment. However, most often the patient was too busy wallowing in the quicksand of denial to seek or accept help. When I, the manager or trainer, extended a branch of help, offering to pull the person out of the quagmire, the salesperson denied needing help. Nothing is wrong. "What's the fuss? I'm okay," the salesperson exclaimed. All the while, the problem grew worse, finally ending what had been a promising career.

The malady suffered, the disease that scuttles so many sales careers, can be rooted in the fear of self-promotion in one or more forms. The fear of self-promotion, also known as *contact hesitation*, prevents salespeople from doing the very things they know are necessary to succeed.

Until recently, contact hesitation, to most sales managers and trainers, translated into the simple fear of rejection: "Your problem is you're just afraid of the word *no*! Don't you know the prospect can't hurt you?" the "old school" sales manager belched as he chewed on a cigar.

The age-old fear first materialized at around puberty, like the fear expressed by many youths preventing them from talking with someone they find attractive. While the fear of rejection can be part of the root problem affecting sales call hesitation, behavioral psychologists digging into this affliction have uncovered much more than the simple fear of being told "No."

Depending on who you ask, anywhere between 6 and 12 separate types of contact hesitation have been uncovered, six or more very different psychological afflictions that, if allowed to, can and will ruin the most promising sales careers.

Furthermore, studies have revealed that contact hesitation is not a problem affecting just new entrants into the sales field. While it's true that up to 80 percent of all salespeople fail within the first year due to insufficient prospecting activity, 40 percent of experienced, successful sales professionals will experience one or more bouts of contact hesitation, hampering their prospecting activity seriously enough to threaten their continuation in sales despite their years of experience, product knowledge, or current income levels. If, however, they learn to cope with and overcome these bouts with contact hesitation, their careers will suffer no permanent damage. If not, their names will be added to the ever-growing list of once successful salespeople.

Contact hesitation is a career-threatening condition that limits what salespeople achieve by emotionally limiting the number of sales calls they make. Some have trouble using the phone to prospect, while others have trouble calling on friends or relatives or important people.

Recently I had the opportunity to test 10 salespeople using a test designed to uncover contact hesitation, along with other factors that could affect the ability to perform as a salesperson in the security field. I asked the sales managers who agreed to have their salespeople tested to place a number where the test asked for a name. I informed the sales managers that, after the testing and evaluation, I would call them to describe their salespeople based on what the test told me.

After evaluating the tests, I called each manager and described the people from that company who had been tested. In each case, the evaluation described the salesperson who took the test quite accurately. As with any testing like this, there were some areas of uncertainty. However, for the most part, the test revealed the person.

Interestingly, when I was speaking with one of the managers describing his salesperson, the test revealed that the salesperson was reluctant to make sales contact with friends and relatives and with people who were perceived to be important or smarter than the salesperson saw himself. The test basically concluded the salesperson would find it more difficult to sell to the president of a company, a doctor, a lawyer, or the like.

In response to the assessment, the manager mentioned that this particular salesperson was one of the top performers. On further checking we found that the salesperson in fact was successful; however, he had accomplished success by working around his problem. He hadn't sold to anyone who was a friend or family member and he avoided calling on people he perceived as more important.

Fortunately for this salesperson, his field of sales allowed him to succeed in spite of his hesitation problem. Were he employed by a division of the company that required he call on presidents of banks, directors of business, lawyers, or others of a higher socioeconomic background, his contact hesitation problem could be a career buster. Armed with this information about a salesperson, the sales manager could plan a program designed to eliminate contact hesitation thus helping the salesperson rise to a higher level of success.

Over the next few pages, we'll explore six of the more common contact hesitation types and attempt to clearly identify each. We'll study examples of each, attempting to paint a picture we all can recognize as we gaze into our own personal life's mirror. We'll attempt to understand the debilitating nature of each type of contact hesitation and search for medicines to fight the disease and finally vaccines to prevent them from occurring.

Your part of the process is to study each with an open mind. Lock yourself in your room, office, or cubicle and, as you read, ask yourself honestly, "Could this be me? Could this be someone working for me?" Ask yourself, "Is my career on track? Am I, and my salespeople, enjoying the success we're capable of? Are we the best we can be? Or, do we need a checkup from the neck up?"

Remember, there is nothing shameful in needing help. There is nothing shameful or career busting about having one or more forms of contact hesitation. The only way contact hesitation in any form is career busting is if it is shrouded in denial, if it is allowed to grow and fester unchecked.

5

Battlefield Phobias

CONTACT HESITATION

Where does contact hesitation come from? The origins of contact hesitation are varied and complex. Some forms appear to be hereditary predispositions. Others can be traced to early traumatic sales experiences. However, most often, contact hesitation is taught *unintentionally* by the sales training process itself. It can be present at the onset of one's sales career or strike years later without warning.

According to the book, *Earning What You're Worth: The Psychology of Sales Reluctance* (Dudley, Goodson, Barnett 1995), all behaviors, including contact hesitation, originate from one of the following sources:

- *Instincts.* These are inclinations and reflexes you were born with. They are automatic tendencies you did not learn and were not taught.
- *Mimic Learning.* As you grew up, you discovered things you could do. These are behaviors you observed in

other people, discovered you could do yourself, and then decided to mimic. Some of the behaviors we exhibit were learned or mimicked when we were very young, often too young to remember today.

- *Passive Learning.* Habits and behavioral styles are unintentionally absorbed from people with whom you regularly interact. These are repeated, predictable behaviors you picked up from parents, teachers, sales trainers, managers, associates, and others without realizing it.
- *Education and Training.* You were purposely taught mannerisms, actions, and behaviors.

Let's look at a couple of case studies. The names in the case studies have been made up; however, in most cases, they represent individuals I have worked with or know of in the sales field.

CASE STUDY 1. BILL

Bill entered the office, rushing past the sales manager's office on his way to his desk. As he passed, Bill breathed a sigh of relief, John, the sales manager, was on the phone and hadn't noticed him.

At his desk now, Bill scanned the all too few phone messages in his in basket. Nothing looked promising. A couple of callbacks from existing customers but no leads, no sales.

Bill knew what he must do but just couldn't get himself to do it. He needed to get off his seat and on the street. Bill needed to make some cold calls. With less than 50 percent of his quota reached and only four days left in the month, Bill felt like a failure and was sure his manager would agree. However, next month would be better, Bill assured himself. Next month the leads would improve and some of the proposals he had out would close.

Just then John entered the sales room. "How's it going Bill?" John asked.

"Great!" Bill lied. "I have several real promising proposals out that should take me over quota for the month."

"The month is almost over," John said, "do you think you'll get the sales in by month's end?"

"It looks real good," Bill said as he glanced at his watch. "Got to run, I don't want to be late for my appointment. I'm scheduled to call on Acme builders. They build over 100 homes a year, and I've got a shot at their security business."

Bill lied. He didn't have an appointment with Acme Builders. The fact is Bill made one call on Acme. And when the receptionist said no one was available to speak with him, Bill gave her his card and asked her to call if they were ever in need of security for their homes. Bill never called back.

Twenty minutes later, as Bill sipped coffee at the local Denny's, he wondered if he could get a job at the shipyard. They might have an opening in marketing for an experienced salesperson. "The security alarm business is just not for me. How can I compete with the giveaways the competition is promoting?" he thought. "I'm just in the wrong business."

Bill, an experienced, once successful salesperson, has a problem. Nothing is wrong with the industry he is in. Nothing is wrong with the company or product Bill represents. The problem resides in Bill. Bill may suffer from one or more forms of contact hesitation. Deep down inside, Bill knows he has a problem. However, he doesn't know how to fix it and he is too embarrassed to ask for help. He certainly won't ask for help from his sales manager. He feels sure he'd get fired if he admitted his problem.

Bill is hesitant to make the sales calls he needs to make even though he knows his future in sales depends on it. When he attempts to make cold calls, he becomes nervous and uncomfortable. He feels as if he is imposing on people who expressed no desire to see him. He knows he should make cold calls; however, at the same time, he feels making such cold calls is unprofessional. He prefers to work with clients who have expressed a need for the product, prospects with whom he can develop a relationship over a period of time, winning the right to do business. Cold calls conflict with his vision of professional selling.

What form of contact hesitation does he suffer? Without testing for them, it's hard to say. He could be suffering from empathizer contact hesitation. The empathizer is characterized by a need to gain the appreciation and approval of everyone, which often results in indecisiveness and conflict avoidance. Empathizers do not prospect well. They may become immobilized by a fear of rejection or disapproval. They may develop an acute sensitivity to interrupting people. Empathizers enjoy servicing existing accounts more than aggressively developing new business. They typically do not like putting themselves into any situation that could cause someone else to be uncomfortable with them. Their extreme conflict avoidance makes it difficult for them to close sales. They prefer that the customer control the sales process. For all these reasons, making cold calls for business is avoided.

CASE STUDY 2. SUZY

Suzy has been selling for Superior Home Improvement for over three years and has enjoyed moderate success. She knows her product and is passionate about the need for professionally installed energy-efficient windows. However, Suzy lags behind most of the other salespeople in her company. Even salespeople who started well after her and admittedly are not as knowledgeable as she regularly outperform her.

During a sales meeting, Suzy's sales manager asked one of the newer salespeople, Melissa, how she'd managed to get going so quick. Melissa's sales were even with Suzy after only working six months for the company. Melissa's reply was that, shortly after getting the job, she did as the sales trainer suggested. She mailed a short announcement note to everyone she knew informing them of her employment with Superior. Once again, as instructed, she followed up each letter with a personal phone call asking for their assistance. The notes and calls paid off. She began getting leads from friends and relatives.

As Suzy listened to Melissa's story, she said to herself, "No way! No way will I involve my family and friends. I haven't till now, and I won't in the future."

Why did Suzy feel as she did? What is so horrible or distasteful about calling on friends or relatives? Suzy apparently feels there is a problem with it. Do you?

Suzy suffers from two contact style problems within contact hesitation. First, she suffers with the hesitation to call on friends. She is emotionally resistant to mixing business interests with friendships. Salespeople with this malady find it difficult to prospect for sales among personal friends or even to ask them for referrals. She avoids even telling friends about what she does for fear of the perception she was attempting to sell them.

Second, she is hesitant to call on family members. She is emotionally resistant to mix business and family. Salespeople with this problem find it extremely difficult, if not impossible, to prospecting for new business among family members or even ask them for referrals. Suzy feels this way despite her firm belief in her product and the need for it.

How did Suzy acquire these career-limiting psychological maladies? Was she born with them? Were they developed through her training? Did management in her company subliminally suggest them. Had she suffered an earlier traumatic sales experience that causes her to feel as she does?

People aren't born with the fear of calling on or selling to friends or family. That feeling is acquired, taught by people whose opinion they respect. Sometimes, the training program at work or one or more of the other influences could have planted the seed that now limits her career.

Well-intentioned sales trainers can plant the seed in how they suggest salespeople develop new sales opportunities. Management can pass along the tendency. And, certainly, a negative sales experience, perhaps with a friend or relative attempting to sell to her or a former sales career whose entire focus was hiring salespeople to sell to friends and relatives, could have planted the deeply rooted seeds of her contact hesitation.

CASE STUDY 3. MANNY

Manny is pleased with himself. He just closed his second sale of the day and is well on his way to a record month in sales. Mr. Simpson is writing a deposit check and Ms. Simpson, as Manny instructed, is glancing through her personal phone directory looking for referral names to give Manny. Life is good.

After giving Manny the name, address, and phone number of three of the Simpson's friends, Ms. Simpson says, "Here's one you should definitely call. If anyone needs and can afford a security system, this family is it. Call our family doctor, his name is Dr. Rufus Peabody. I'm sure after hearing what you told us today, he'll get one."

As with the other names given by Ms. Simpson, Manny writes Dr. Peabody's name on his referral form.

Later at his office, Manny begins the process he's become so accustomed to, and frankly, he doesn't mind telling you, a process he is very good at. He calls the first name on the list. After explaining why he's calling, Manny asks for a convenient appointment time. The prospect at first says she's not interested, which of course Manny expected. Manny goes on to explain why she would benefit from the appointment even if she didn't buy. After a couple of objections, countered by good sense answers, the prospect agrees to the appointment. On hanging up the phone, Manny yells, "Yes!" For Manny knows, all too well, if he can get the appointment he'll sell over 70 percent of the time.

Manny continues on to the second and then third name with similar results. The last name on the list is Dr. Peabody. However, unlike the previous calls, as Manny dials Dr. Peabody's phone number he begins to grow tense. His hands begin to sweat just a little and his throat constricts. The Peabody's maid answers the phone. In an almost inaudible voice Manny asks to speak to Dr. or Ms. Peabody. Ms. Peabody comes to the phone and Manny once again explains the purpose of his call. However, this time he's not smiling. This time he's not so self-assured. His voice even appears to be a bit squeaky as he attempts to set an appointment. When Ms. Peabody says she is not interested, thank you very much, Manny thanks her and hangs up the phone. No attempt is made to answer the objection. No good sense answer is prompted by the expected objection. Just, thanks anyway and good-bye.

What happened? What happened to the self-assured, professional salesperson who just minutes earlier completed three successful calls? To someone listening in on the calls, the last call sounded like it was made by someone else. Someone impersonating the supersalesperson Manny.

What happened is a common case of contact hesitation, which is characterized by the emotional hesitation to make contact with up-market prospective buyers, people of importance and/or social standing—doctors, lawyers, and Indian chiefs. Socially self-conscious salespeople are intimidated by persons of wealth, prestige, or power. Their once self-assured persona crumbles into a mousy, weak, submissive shell of a salesperson.

Salespeople like Manny hide their contact hesitation by a verbalized, overcavalier disregard for status. They'll proclaim their ability to call on and sell to anyone. However, their actions and record will say something entirely different.

CASE STUDY 4. JIM

Jim has worked for World Alarm Protection (WAP), a very large security alarm service company, for over 15 years. His job is selling residential security systems to homeowners. Although relatively successful, he has not reached the levels he feels he should reach and advancement has completely eluded him.

Throughout his years with WAP, Jim has been assigned to a territory on the opposite side of the large city in which he was born and raised. Consequently, he's had no reason or opportunity to sell to family members.

Jim's father, a successful doctor, and Jim's brother, an engineer, aren't really sure what Jim does for a living. They, of course, know he works for WAP, but don't know what Jim does for WAP. Jim never talks about it. When anyone asks, Jim becomes evasive or quickly changes the subject.

One day Jim's grandmother, in reply to a mail solicitation from WAP advertising a special promotion WAP was offering senior citizens, arranged to meet with a salesperson from the company. The sales appointment was scheduled for the next day.

The salesperson arrived as scheduled the following day. After selling Jim's grandmother the system she wanted, she mentioned that her grandson also worked for WAP. "Do you know him," she asked? "His name is Jim Morrison." The salesperson said, "Sure I know Jim, he's in my department, he sells security alarm systems just like me."

Later in the week Jim happened to call his grandmother. When he did, she told him about the sales call from WAP and how the salesperson knew him as he was in the same department. "Jim," his grandmother said, "I didn't know you were in sales, if I had known you sold for WAP I would have called you. I'm sorry." Jim told her it didn't matter, said good-bye, and hung up the phone.

Jim was furious. The next day he approached the salesperson who had sold to his grandmother and said, "How dare you tell my grandmother I'm in sales. No one in my family knows and I don't want them to know."

Jim has a problem. The particular form he suffers from is called sales identity/role aversion. Jim is embarrassed about being a salesperson. He and other salespeople like him go to great extents to mask their true profession. They are ashamed of being in sales, often because they're sure family members and close friends would consider them a failure or, at best, less than successful, because they are in sales.

Sales identity/role aversion has been found to be extremely contagious and characterized by unexpressed and unresolved guilt and shame about being in sales. Role averse salespeople hide their profession behind other titles to avoid being labeled a salesperson.

Sales managers and trainers have been identified as the primary carriers of sales identity hesitation. Salespeople who have been exposed to a role averse sales management team, according to a study referenced in *Earning What You're Worth, The Psychology of Sales Call Reluctance*, are 20 times more likely to have toxic levels of sales identity role aversion.

CASE STUDY 5. BECKY

Stan Farber, sales manager for World Automation Systems (WAS), receives a phone call from one of his good customers, Karen Philippe, to whom he sold a rather complete home automation system four years earlier. After exchanging niceties, Stan learns the reason for Karen's call. Karen is in the process of adding a study, bath, and playroom onto her house and would like to have a representative of WAS look over the plans to add to her existing automation system.

Because of Stan's very busy schedule, he asked Karen if it would be acceptable to send an associate in his place. Karen agreed on the condition the associate see her within the next 24 hours, as the job was moving quite fast and sheetrock was scheduled to be installed within the next day or two.

Stan calls Becky, one of his newer sales associates, into his office to give her the lead. Stan explains that the existing system is the same basic model they sell now, one Becky is familiar with. He further explains that what Karen wants is basic and no problem to add onto the existing system. However, Stan makes it clear that timing is critical, as the sheetrock is due to be installed within the next day or two, and with the time it takes to schedule the addition, considering WAS's already busy schedule, she needs to see the prospect today.

Becky takes notes as Stan explains the situation. Three hours later, Stan walks through the sales office and sees Becky seated at her desk going through a stack of papers.

> Stan: "When are you going to Karen's to look over her plans for the addition?"
>
> Becky: "I wanted to look through Karen's file first before going."
>
> Stan: "As I said to you when I gave you this lead, the system is our basic system, there is no problem adding to it, and Karen needs you there today."
>
> Becky: "Okay, I'm about finished anyway."

An hour or so later, Stan passes the service area and sees Becky showing paperwork to the service manager.

> Stan: "Is that the addition for Karen Philippe?"
>
> Becky: "No, this is the original paperwork. I wanted to make sure service wouldn't have a problem with the additional work before going to see Karen."
>
> Stan: "Are you saying you haven't *seen Karen* yet? I gave you that lead hours ago and told you how urgent it was."

Stan was obviously upset, and Becky didn't understand why. She was going to handle the call just as soon as she was sure she had all the facts.

Is this a case of contact hesitation? The form of contact hesitation Becky suffers is analyzer call hesitation. Analyzers are data sensitive. This style is characterized by a need to collect, analyze, and disseminate information. Analyzers may be overly detail conscious or technically oriented. Their prospecting efforts may be severely limited by constant overpreparation and perfectionism. They may delay or default on making sales calls because of relatively minor problems, like typographical errors on reports or not feeling able to answer every question that a prospect might ask. Analyzers are more interested in collecting and analyzing data than in aggressively developing new business. They typically enjoy designing customer contact procedures more than actually contacting customers. They are emotionally aloof and prefer the company of computers to people.

Analyzers like Becky spend more time gathering information and data than in front of prospects. They can't seem to be prepared enough, so they look for other facts and figures so they can be 100 percent sure before facing the prospect. The obvious limiting factor of this type of contact hesitation is they make too few calls, wasting precious selling time gathering unneeded data. While Becky vacillates about going on the appointment, critical time is lost and, all too often, the sale is lost to a competitor.

CASE STUDY 6. MEL

Mel is a relatively new salesperson with World Office Equipment Systems. He has received some initial product training as well as a five-day "quick start" training course, covering a variety of subjects, including sales presentation skills, prospecting, system design, and closing skills. Mel has made some sales; however, he's not exactly setting sales records in comparison to other salespeople with equal tenure.

Today Mel is in attendance at a required sales training meeting, focusing on the skill of handling objections and closing sales. Mel knows he needs better closing skills but he tells himself that he's sure the methods presented will be ones he cannot see himself using because they will violate his feeling of what professionals should do. Mel has attended other sales training meetings and came to the very conclusion he now fears will be repeated.

At the beginning of the training, the trainer asks the group to list the objections most frequently heard from prospects that, left unanswered, would likely eliminate the possibility of making the sale on that call.

After a list of some 8 or 10 objections surfaced, the trainer took each one and suggested methods to answer and thus eliminate it. While other salespeople attending the training took notes, Mel systematically took issue with each method for every objection.

In the name of playing "devil's advocate," Mel claimed each was ineffective because if he were the prospect he wouldn't appreciate the salesperson using the tactic. Each method in Mel's opinion was pushy, hard sell, and would expose the salesperson to the prospect as trying to force the sale, something Mel didn't want his prospect to feel.

Other salespeople in attendance disagreed with Mel's assessment and told him so. Some gave examples of times they used the method being taught and were successful in getting the sale. But Mel remained steadfast in his feelings.

When asked, Mel agreed that probably less than 1 in 50 prospects would feel as he does; however, Mel still objected and constantly interrupted, challenged, or argued with the trainer throughout the meeting, always justifying his commentary as playing devil's advocate.

If one were to interview past managers of salespeople like Mel, they probably would say that they experienced a similar problem with Mel. They would likely say that Mel is uncoachable, untrainable; that Mel constantly disrupts training classes, arguing with the trainer, challenging the validity of what is being taught. Mel is a know-it-all. Research would likely find that Mel was dismissed from or quit other positions for this very reason.

What is Mel's problem? Mel suffers from commander contact hesitation.

Commanders need to be and stay in control. This style is characterized by assertiveness, decisiveness, even intimidation, and perhaps counteraction. Commanders approach customer contact with a predisposition to stay in control of the sales process. This may take the form of resisting or refusing to put themselves in situations where they may feel at a disadvantage. Commanders may become impatient or even critical when prospects or clients don't respond as expected. They resist prospecting as demeaning and will find others to do the prospecting for them. Commanders are extremely competitive and may even intimidate clients into a sale. They may prefer to find new business rather than service existing accounts. These salespeople are emotionally unable to allow themselves to be coached, advised, managed, or trained. Many low to average sales producers remain low to average producers due to this form of contact hesitation. Do you recognize this person?

TESTING FOR CONTACT HESITATION

Just because a prospective salesperson has a mild case of contact hesitation in one of its forms doesn't necessarily mean you shouldn't hire that individual. However, if all you need are three salespeople, one of the four you can hire exhibits contact hesitation and all else is equal, I'd probably hire the three without contact hesitation. You also should test existing salespeople to determine where they may need help.

At the present time I'm aware of only two assessments concentrating on behaviors that affect selling such as contact hesitation. One has been around a long time: SPQ*GOLD, the Call Reluctance Scale. Written by psychologists (not salespeople), it is very clinical and requires special training to administer and use. It assesses social phobias.

The other assessment is relatively new and capitalizes on new insights in brain physiology and perceptual psychology. Contact Styles Survey (CSS) is published by PsychoMetrics International, Dallas, Texas. It was developed by Dr. David Barnett, who, in addition to academic knowledge, knows the ups and downs of professional selling. CSS is more flexible, easier to understand, and does not require special training or certification.

THE PERSONAL INTERVIEW

Testing does not replace a good personal interview. Armed with the results from the test, you can structure questions aimed at weaknesses the test may have uncovered.

Here are a few questions I like to ask of new applicants that help me in the selection process:

1. *According to your application, you previously worked for ABC company. What did you like most about working for ABC?* Listen carefully to the answers. I would hope the applicant can find something good to say about his or her experiences at ABC. The answer could tell me if the applicant tends to see the glass half full or half empty.

2. *What did you like least about ABC?* This answer could give you a preview of what you'll be facing when managing this person.

3. *Tell me about something you've accomplished so far in life of which you are particularly proud.*

4. *Tell me about a time when you succeeded when the odds were somewhat stacked against you.*

5. *Tell me about a time when you were given the responsibility to accomplish a task from start to finish.*

6. *If we hire you, we will provide training on our products and services, tell me the first three or four steps you'd take to ensure your success with our company.*

7. *If we hire you, what do you expect us to do for you to assist you in reaching your personal goals?*

8. *Is there anything you believe could hinder your success with our company?*

9. *Your application says you earned $30,000 last year. How much are you hoping to make the first year with*

our company? Let's assume the applicant answers $40,000.

10. *Let's assume you make the $40,000 goal you're setting for yourself. What would you do with the extra $10,000 you make? How would it change your life?* Don't let the applicant give you a fuzzy answer, such as "It would make me happier." Get the applicant to tell you exactly what he or she would use the money for: a car, a down payment on a home, a boat, a vacation, an annuity, what?

All of these question are open-ended, designed to get the applicant to talk. They help uncover the salesperson's attitude, goals, and aspirations, as well as personal goals I can use to motivate the salesperson after he or she is hired, such as the new car.

THE BACKGROUND CHECK

While a background check is important, don't expect too much from it. Previous employers rarely complete employment forms you send them. And, if they do, they'll rarely give you more than the dates employed and possibly income earned.

If I can speak with the applicant's previous manager, I can structure questions about the applicant that are easier for the previous manager to answer without feeling that by doing so he or she is in danger of being sued:

1. Your previous employee said he or she was employed by your company between __ and __. Is that about right?
2. He or she said the position held with (duties at) your company was __. Is that correct?
3. He or she listed earnings of approximately __. Is that about right?

4. We're interviewing this applicant for a sales position. The position we are filling requires [or does not require] the applicant to have previous sales experience. If you had a similar opening within your company, would you rehire this person?

5. If the employee reapplied for the position he or she vacated and the position was open, would you rehire him or her?

These questions provide some of the information a previous employer could give me to help with the hire. If the employer wouldn't hire the applicant for a sales position, I'd ask why, in hopes of an honest answer. If the employer wouldn't rehire the applicant if the same position previously held was available, I'd also ask why.

GUT INSTINCT

At the end of it all, you're back to your gut instinct. This is great, if you've had a lot of experience hiring good salespeople in the field you're in. If not, it takes time and failure to develop the instincts needed.

Ask yourself these questions about the candidate:

1. If I were one of my prospects, would I open my door to the person sitting across from me now?

2. If I were a prospect, would I believe what this person says to me?

3. If I were a prospect, would I buy from this person?

4. If I were a prospect, would I refer this person to my friends and relatives?

5. As the employer, would I want the person sitting across from me, representing my company?

If you answered no to any of these questions, pass. Don't hire the applicant. That's your gut talking to you.

6

Behavioral Study

Dr. Eden Ryl, a behavioral psychologist, compared a sales-person's hesitancy or fear to make a sales call to her own personal fears of height and water. Such fear, while appearing silly or stupid to some, is debilitating to those who suffer it. Dr. Ryl's personal cure was to study sky diving, to learn all she could from professionals about how to safely jump from an airplane and land safely in the ocean.

Her video, *Pack Your Own Chute*, a Ramic Productions Film, takes the viewer through every phase of chute technology, de-sign, and packing. The video shows Dr. Ryl taking sky diving lessons, learning how to jump, how and when to pull the chute release, what to do if the first chute release doesn't work, how to control the direction of descent, and how to hit the ground and fall correctly.

The point Dr. Ryl makes for salespeople in her video is that, to undertake something you fear, you should first study the steps involved until you completely understand what it takes. Work with a professional in whom you believe, one who knows how to do it. Practice on the ground in a safe environment before taking the plunge. Mentally prepare for the jump (the presentation) before you actually do it. Then, pack your own chute before jumping. In other words, make the program yours, get comfortable with the words you'll use, before sharing it with your prospect.

As discussed previously, it is not unusual for a salesperson, for whatever reason, to suffer somewhat from career limiting contact hesitation. However, the key is in knowing the problem exists. You can't fix what you're not aware is broken.

As in the example of the salesperson who is a top producer yet is limited by the fear of contacting friends and relatives, we must first uncover the weakness, then put into motion a plan designed to correct the weakness.

After recognizing which contact hesitation or behavioral style is limiting you or your salesperson, it is time to begin questioning the source of the career-limiting beliefs. We must break it down into small pieces, analyzing each piece individually, searching for the root cause. Then, we must determine how we can perform the task at hand without the debilitating feelings that previously accompanied it. We must analyze the feelings we have and question their right to hold us hostage.

When I was in my mid-twenties, a few months after I got married, I discovered I had a fear of height, acrophobia. I hadn't been afraid of height in the past. I spent four years on an aircraft carrier and walked the catwalks high above the water with no fear. I climbed trees, walked on rooftops, and rode on roller coasters and Ferris wheels.

However, one Saturday afternoon as I stepped into my backyard, with the intention of cutting a branch from a tree that was partially broken by high winds, as I took the third step up the ladder, an uncontrollable sense of fear came over me. I couldn't take the next step. I was frozen in place, not at all understanding why I felt as I did.

From that day forward for several years, my fear of height grew worse. I couldn't approach and close a window if that window was on the second floor or higher. I couldn't walk on a roof. I couldn't even stand by a fixed plate glass window in a high rise building. I grew angrier and angrier with myself and was determined to eliminate the fear.

Little by little I attempted to change the fear. I thought back to when I wasn't afraid and searched for the reason I began to fear height. During one of my soul searches I remember the incident that gave birth to my fear.

The day after I got married, Debbie and I went on our honeymoon to the Pocono Mountains. To get to the resort required we travel the last 50 to 75 miles up the mountain by bus. Without considering anything but the improved view, we sat in the seats in the very front of the bus. The driver, who probably had driven the 50 or so miles every day for the past 10 years, drove fast. As we careened around hairpin turns, the bus seemed to hang over the edge of the road. The drop from that point was probably hundreds of feet, however, to us below sea level newlyweds, it seemed more like thousands of feet.

I don't recall being terrified by the experience, but a small spot in my brain must have been and recorded the fear to arise some months later. Once I came to grips with from where the fear originated, coupled with the logical fact that it was unlikely I'd fall out of a window by simply closing it, my fear gradually subsided.

The fearful feelings some salespeople get when sitting with an upscale client is very much like the fear of height I suffered. It is just as debilitating and makes as little sense. However, it is very real.

Salespeople also program themselves or are programmed by others to accept as fact other things that are just not true. Logical or not, they believe them. There is a saying that, "when logic comes in conflict with emotions, emotions always win."

Dr. Ryl also demonstrated how our minds and what we believe is true affect what we can and will do. So much so, that we actually will go to our graves with the beliefs we hold sacred, right or wrong, fact or fiction.

In a demonstration using a Northern pike, a voracious eater, Dr. Ryl vividly demonstrated the power of our mind and beliefs. A Northern pike was placed in an aquarium. A cupful of the pike's favorite food, small minnowlike fish, was poured into the aquarium with the pike. In a blurring eating frenzy, the Northern pike quickly devoured the fish.

Next, a clear cylinder was lowered into the tank and some more fish poured inside the cylinder, out of reach of the pike. Immediately, the pike attacked the fish it saw but to no avail. The fish were inside the cylinder the pike couldn't see. The pike attacked again and again. Little by little, its enthusiasm dimmed, until it quit attacking altogether. It now was convinced, try as it might, that the fish it saw could not be eaten. After some time had passed since his last attempted attack, the cylinder was lifted out of the water leaving the fish in the tank to swim where they wanted. The fish swam by the pike. Nothing happened. The pike didn't attack. The fish swam up to the pike, feeding on algae from around its mouth and eyes. Nothing happened. The pike did not attack. The pike eventually died of starvation with its favorite food swimming all around it.

This happened because the pike came to the conclusion, after numerous attempts and tiring effort, that the fish accompanying it in the tank could not be eaten. Even though this no longer was true and, under the circumstances, illogical, the pike believed the programmed conditioning it was subjected to. The pike was convinced and went to its grave with its belief.

Like the pike, sometimes salespeople internalize a personal experience programming their brain (personal computer) to believe what happened is what will happen every time. Now that's a great thing to do to yourself if what happens as a result of what you do is a positive event. It's another story when the result is negative.

Many failing and weak salespeople have programmed their computer to believe the prospect won't say yes at the point of a presentation without a few days or more to think it over. So, with this belief controlling their actions, the salesperson doesn't ask the customer to buy. The salesperson doesn't attempt even the easiest of closing questions.

A couple of years ago, when I was responsible for managing salespeople located in the 10 offices of a large alarm company, the company conducted a survey, taken after each trainee went home after training. The salesperson was instructed to call 10 alarm companies in his or her area and tell each company he or she was interested in buying an alarm system. Our salesperson asked the representative from the rival company to come to his or her home after 5 PM and before 10 PM, on any day that was convenient, Monday through Friday. We didn't even ask the competitor's salesperson to go to an appointment on weekend days or nights, just weekdays.

The result of the study was as follows. On average, only 6 of the 10 companies with whom appointments were made actually arrived for the appointment. Four didn't bother to show up. Ask yourself why? Why wouldn't four companies' salespeople, on average, arrive for an appointment when the prospect said he or she was interested in buying an alarm system?

Of the six salespeople who did arrive for the appointment, only one, on average, asked the prospect to buy the product, only one attempted to close the sale. The remaining salespeople left a quote, verbally quoted a price, or offered to mail a quotation in a few days.

Why? Why did the company representative go through all the time and effort to go see the prospect and then not ask the prospect to buy the product?

I suspect it's because the salesperson went on the sales call with the predisposition that the prospect would not buy at the completion of the presentation, with the belief the prospect would want to spend some time thinking it over. Why bother asking a question to which the answer already is known? Like the pike, the salesperson's personal programming held that asking for the order was a waste of time and energy. And, like the pike, many salespeople starve to death in sales as a result of their negative programming.

Some salespeople have attempted to prospect by phone, with bad results. Other salespeople have attempted to make sales by knocking on doors and had bad results. Still others attempted to develop a network of bird dogs and experienced negative results. And even others attempted to gather referrals immediately after a sale and failed to get them. These salespeople allowed themselves to believe that asking for the order is a waste of time, not worth doing. They programmed their personal computers with these erroneous facts, and the damage was done. Garbage in, garbage out. And, like the pike, their careers starve because of the belief they allow to reside within their minds.

You cannot act in conflict with your own self-image. What you believe is true will be true for you. Success and the feeling, "I am and will always be successful," is a programmed belief.

Change your self-image, check your beliefs, portray the correct image, and you'll change your life.

7

Boot Camp—Don't Blame the Untrained

Once you have a good picture of the type sales candidates you are seeking and a fair idea of how you might locate them, it is time to plan what you're going to do with them once they are hired. No one will argue that it costs money to recruit and retain good salespeople. So it should follow that we must do all we can to ensure that the investment we make in finding good people isn't wasted.

You must come to grips with a piece of reality: Salespeople need and want training. I don't care how much experience one has, ongoing training is important to selling success. Without training, even the best get lazy or lose some of their luster in selling. Sometimes, all we need is a half-day sales class that reminds us about all of the things we already know but either quit using or forgot.

It never ceases to amaze me at the sales seminars I give, watching sales professionals slap themselves on the side of their heads as I point out a sales technique they used at one time or another but, for some reason unknown even to themselves, quit doing, techniques that worked well for them in the past. Sales training for true professionals is a great reminder or refresher. And, sometimes, they learn something entirely new. The fact is, I learn from the seminar participants almost every time I conduct a seminar.

The type and scope of training you should provide the new sales candidate depends on the type sales organization you're putting together: whether you will be addressing the custom market, selling products for upwards of $2000, or marketing low-end security alarms; and how your salesperson gets to the prospect—telemarketing (being handed leads or personally developing them), knocking on doors, self-generation through direct mail, or bird dogging. One thing is certain, you cannot just turn the salespeople lose and expect success. The odds are strong against you if you do.

THE TRAINING

The type training you employ depends largely on the side of the business you enter: high end or low end. If you choose to specialize in the high end, salespeople must receive more training because

1. The jobs are bigger and more complicated.
2. The number of product types installed increases, necessitating more product knowledge.
3. The sale amount is much higher, requiring better closing skills.
4. The prospect often is more affluent and educated, requiring a more thorough presentation.

If you choose to sell to the low-end market, less training is needed, because package selling makes the product knowledge easier to learn and lower price points are closed more easily. The following is an outline of a seven-day training class suitable for high-end sales.

HIGH-END SALES TRAINING PROGRAM
Training Day 1

About the Industry   To know where you are going, historians always have taught, it is best to know where you've been. For the first part of the first day, we spend a little time understanding from where the industry came and how it has affected the things we attempt to do today. Also, high-end salespeople will find themselves visiting clients who already have the company's product, often an older version, that they wish to update. This requires knowledge of some of the products the company previously sold.

The Psychological Law of Self-Exception   When you ask industry professionals—or anyone who has sold security alarms for over six months—what percentage of the population in any community needs an alarm system, the answer always is "everyone." However, the fact remains that less than 20 percent of households have an alarm system. Therefore, the consumer obviously doesn't agree.

However, everything changes when a burglar strikes. The households without an alarm now know they need an alarm system. The psychological law of self-exception causes people to read an ad for an alarm system and comment to themselves that the purchase seems reasonable and if they needed one they'd buy it. They know other people who should buy one but not themselves.

It is important salespeople understand this psychological law so that they understand, when a prospect says he or she doesn't need an alarm system, it isn't necessarily so. They just don't know they need one.

The Buyer's Wall of Resistance   Next, it is important for salespeople to face all of the concerns, emotions, feelings, and objections that prevent the prospect making a decision during the appointment. They have to understand the prospect's objections and learn how to overcome them.

The Problem   If they are to be effective, the salespeople must know and understand the problems the product or service solves. They must become consultants, doctors, of the services offered. They must learn how to explain the problem to a potential client without the explanation sounding like a scare tactic.

Training Days 2–4

Day 1 introduces and begins the eight step selling plan.

1. *The Warm-Up.* Time is spent teaching salespeople how to do an effective warm-up, followed by videotaped role playing.
2. *Sell Yourself.* People buy from people. In the direct selling field, where customers see the salespeople in their homes, not in a store, the salesperson *is* the company. How the customer feels about the salesperson, will, most likely, be how the customer feels about the company the salesperson represents. So it is important to explain what you as a salesperson bring to the purchase. What experience do you have that should prove beneficial to the prospect? How long have you been a security consultant? What type(s) of training have you received? What is your personal commitment to the customer's satisfaction after the sale is made?
3. *Selling the Company.* Salespeople must learn how to demonstrate to the prospect the advantages of doing business with their company, the benefits the prospect will enjoy when selecting that company over the competition.

4. *Establish Need*. Salespeople must learn the questions to ask that determine the prospect's need for the product and services.

Day 2 is spent learning the first three steps of the sale, role playing each step and videotaping each trainee in selling situations. We play back, discuss, and critique each role play. If time permits, we videotape a second round of role playing, including playing it back and critiquing. Salespeople get a lot out of videotaped role playing. They see themselves in action, probably for the first time. And they see real improvement between the first and second rounds of role playing.

This form continues throughout these three days. Steps 1–3 are worked on during Day 1; steps 4 and 5 on Day 2; and steps 6 and 7 on Day 3.

5. *The Selling Survey*. Salespeople must learn how to conduct a selling survey that involves the prospects. Designing a security system for a home or business is not simply a case of counting windows and doors to determine the price. Designing a system requires thought and concern for the way the prospect uses their home or business. How they move about. When they come and go. Design also concerns pets, small children, work schedules, etc. As you walk through the prospect's home you should take note of security challenges and present them to the prospect. Ask questions such as, *"How do you feel about this window? I notice the back of your yard is surrounded by an eight foot privacy fence, this, of course, makes it easier for a burglar to work on getting in the home from the back without being noticed."* A good selling survey is full of trial closes, such as *"Mrs. Jones, when the system is installed, would it be more convenient for the system touch pad, which is used to arm or disarm the system, be installed close to the front door, or would the side garage door be a better location for you?"*

6. *Explain the Problem.* To ensure that the prospect buys for the right reason and is adequately protected, it is necessary to explain the problems he or she faces. A professional will do this in a way that is educational rather than use scare tactics. Both can result in the sale; however, prospects who feel the salesperson has taken the time to educate him or her will be quick to refer the representative to friends and family.

7. *Demonstrate the Solution.* Salespeople must learn how to demonstrate the products and services the company provides to solve the problems mentioned previously. They must be able to do so in a manner that doesn't confuse the prospect. Using the product or service must be easy and not require the prospect to get help from the next-door neighbor's 10-year-old.

8. *Ask for the Order.* It should be obvious that the reason the salesperson is meeting with the prospect is to see if the prospect is interested in owning the product or service after hearing the evidence presented by the salesperson. If the salesperson doesn't ask for the order, how can he or she expect to make the sale. Nine out of 10 salespeople, according to a survey I conducted, do not ask a closing question at the end of their presentation. Rather, they put together a proposal, an estimate, or simply tell the prospect how much the product or service will cost and then leave without asking if the prospect would like to proceed. There is little doubt that we must teach salespeople we hire to comfortably ask for the order on every presentation made.

Selling the solution, which is the demonstration of the product, requires time. We must be sure the salesperson is able to explain the product in a fashion that appears simple to the prospect. The last thing we want to do is confuse the prospect.

Training Day 5. Closing the Sale

Training Day 5 is devoted to handling objections commonly heard in sales. We watch a video, *Handling Objections and Closing the Sale,*[1] which clearly demonstrates the proper way to handle objections. The video demonstrates this in a role playing environment. Students get to observe an objection raised and witness an effective close. My book *The Formula for Selling Alarm Systems*[2] and the video and audio series *Handling Objections and Closing the Sale* are extremely effective tools for sales training.

LOW-END SALES TRAINING

It is easier to sell low-end, low-priced systems because of, if for no other reason, price. There is less sales resistance to the offer to install an alarm system for under $200 than when the prospect is expected to fork over $2000. However, selling is selling—still requiring sales skills, a strong work ethic, the ability to live with rejection, and the fortitude to press on every day with minimal supervision.

If the company you plan to put together will focus on the low end, you'll also need to give a lot of thought to the management structure you will have to organize (see Chapters 13 and 14).

Low-end sales necessitates selling in volume. I have worked closely with alarm dealers that, at the time of this writing, are selling more than 1200 systems every month. These organizations are designed to hire salespeople on a weekly, if not daily, basis. They have a training program that is a lot quicker than the one described previously. The entire training is reduced from six days to approximately two days. However, the salespeople they hire enjoy plenty of personal coaching and on-the-job training.

[1] DBS Productions, 888-827-7355.
[2] Boston, MA: Butterworth-Heinemann, 1996.

They also hire people who have never sold before. Like the Kirby vacuum cleaner company I started with many years ago, they look for the diamond in the rough, and evidenced by the sales they make, they find them.

The following is a rough outline of a training plan for a high-volume, low-end, low-price sales group.

Training Day 1

1. Introduce the eight step selling plan (as previously).
2. Hand out presentation books and a script, which follows a plan.
3. Demonstrate how the presentation book is used.
4. Break up into couples and take turns role playing the use of the presentation books.
5. Discuss the package product sold.
6. Discuss prices.
7. Explain how the product works; that is, touch pad, infrared, smoke detector.
8. Break up into groups of two again and role play the product explanation.
9. Break for dinner.
10. Assign homework.
11. Have trainee(s) ride on night appointments with a senior salesperson.

Training Day 2

1. Discuss the preceding night's appointments.
2. List common objections.
3. Show the video *Handling Objections and Closing the Sale*.
4. Discuss the objections and closings presented in video.
5. Break up into groups of two and role play handling an objection.
6. Role play the presentation and closing.
7. Train to handle sales agreements.

8. Break for dinner.
9. Have trainee(s) ride on evening appointments with a senior salesperson.

Day 3

1. The trainee attends a regular sales meeting with senior salespeople.
2. Each trainee is assigned to a team leader.
3. The trainees are taken along with other salespeople to the designated neighborhood for canvassing. The goal is to set three or more appointments for that day or evening.
4. The team leader accompanies the trainee on the first appointments. The trainee does the presentation with team leader observing.
5. After each appointment, the team leader critiques the appointment and coaches the trainee.

Training Day 4

1. The trainee attends a regular sales meeting.
2. The trainee accompanies other salespeople in the field, unless it was determined from the previous night that additional in-house training is required.

Training Day 5

1. The trainee attends a regular sales meeting.
2. The trainee meets with the team leader for personal help and coaching.
3. The trainee works in the field, as before.

All of this training assumes the organization is utilizing door-to-door canvassing for leads. If a telemarketing program is in effect, leads for that day usually are distributed at the meeting.

TRAINING AIDS

Resource material is invaluable in training new people into the business and into sales. Prior to developing my own material, which is a compilation of all of the training I received in the past from sales "gurus" such as Tom Hopkins, Zig Ziglar, and Doug Edwards, I utilized video- and audiotapes produced by them. Because their tapes didn't specifically address the security alarm sales business, I spent some time before the training planning how to convert their training to the alarm business. Then, during training, I played the tapes followed by an alarm business interpretation by me.

My book *The Formula for Selling Alarm Systems* does that for you. It teaches how to sell alarm systems. And, if I do say so myself, *The Formula for Selling Alarm Systems* is the best alarm sales training book available today.

I also have a video- and audiotape training series, *Handling Objections and Closing the Sale.* By using the video in sales training, the trainees will see a role play handling several objections and closing the sale. By giving each salesperson the two-tape audio series, the time they spend in their cars going to and from sales calls can be devoted to education and improving their sales skills.

The Formula for Selling Alarm Systems and *Handling Objections and Closing the Sale* (the two-hour, four-VHS-tapes video series and two-tape audio series) can be ordered from DBS Productions.[3]

---

[3] DBS Productions LLC, #3 Laurus, Littleton, CO 80127; 1-888-827-SELL (7355) toll free phone and fax.

8

Train the Troops to Close the Sale

How many closes should a professional salesperson know? I'm asked this question often, and the answer is an easy one. A true professional should know at least one answer to each of the most common objections a prospect may come up with. A star, a champion salesperson, will know two or three answers for the top three objections and at least two answers for the less common ones.

However, if your salespeople are trained to know at least one answer per objection, they will be better prepared than upwards of 75 percent of salespeople. Sadly, my experience tells me that most salespeople, 75 percent or more, are not prepared to professionally answer the top five objections they face on a regular basis.

Here, we review the objections salespeople in the security alarm field encounter in everyday selling. We further analyze why the prospects might feel as they do and how to answer each objection. Next, we learn how to turn a potential confrontation into a friendly, yet closing conversation.

Some of the most common objections are these:

1. I want to think it over.
2. I want to shop around.
3. Your price is too high.
4. I have a dog.
5. I just don't think I need one.
6. I have a gun and will use it.
7. I have insurance.
8. I have nothing to steal.
9. Someone always is at home.
10. I have good nosy neighbors.

During my 30-year sales and sales management career, I have searched for sales training methods and programs designed to help a person get started and keep going in sales. I learned the hard way that just turning a salesperson loose, with no specific plan or road map for success, left too much to chance and most often was unsuccessful. For this reason I have spent the better part of my career developing sales training programs that work. So, as you sit in your office or at home at the end of your day, do yourself and your career a favor, review this chapter at least six times. Repetition is the mother of learning, so, by reading this chapter six times, you'll etch the training into your mind, making it easier to scan for the words to use in a closing situation when you need answers. As you drive to and from appointments or your office, play one of my audiotapes and listen as I overcome commonly heard objections you face daily in selling.

However, before I go any further, let's make it clear that, with the exception of some tweaking and customizing, I didn't create the closing skills I'm about to share with you. I attended numerous sales training seminars and schools throughout my career. I met great sales trainers who learned their selling skills from trainers they listened to, who learned their selling skills from still others who were kind enough to share those skills. It now is my turn to share these successful selling and closing skills with you.

To start, I'd like to ask you a question. Do you close the sale or are you guilty of just getting close to the sale? The words *close* and *close* are spelled alike yet have entirely different meanings. In sales, the difference can be the difference between eating and starving, success and failure. Zig Ziglar calls the salesperson who gets only close to the sale a *professional visitor*. Getting close to the sale just doesn't count in selling.

So, to ensure you close the sale more often, it's important you analyze those factors that prevent you from closing the sale. We must search for the reasons why prospects stop us from completing the sale. At the same time, we must recognize that the problem well may start in our own minds, in our own pre-conceived notion of how the sales appointment will end.

If you were to analyze the sales process to determine at what point a salesperson becomes a visitor rather than a closer, you likely would conclude that the point occurs when the sales-person fails to ask for the order. If this sounds almost unbeliev-able to you, you must know that the majority of so-called salespeople don't ask for the order. They do everything they were taught to do when meeting with prospective buyers, but stop short at asking for the order. They leave at the end of their presentation without asking the prospect to commit to the purchase. Without giving the prospect an opportunity to say "Yes."

To make my point, a couple of years ago, when I was directly responsible for managing and training salespeople working in several different cities throughout the United States, I conducted surveys at the end of each initial training class. The surveys conducted were as follows.

At the end of training I instructed the trainees, over the next couple of days, to call 10 competitor companies and make an appointment for a representative of that company to go to their homes to sell them the product. To be sure the test was consistent, we provided the trainee with a basic script, outlining the exact words to use when making the appointment.

Our sales trainees were instructed to speak to a salesperson of the company they were calling and to tell the company's sales rep that he or she was interested in buying. However, since both the trainee and his or her spouse worked during the day, the appointment had to be scheduled for after 5 PM and before 10 PM any day it was convenient, Monday through Friday. We didn't even ask the company rep to work on weekends, just on weeknights.

The results of our study is as follows. Out of 10 companies called, on average, only 6 showed up for the appointment. Four didn't even arrive even when they had a definite appointment.

Before we go any further, we have to ask ourselves, "Why? Why would four company sales reps, who had definite appointments with prospects who said they were interested in buying, not show up for the appointment? What was going through their minds? Did they have too much business already and weren't interested in more? Had they already made too much money that year and were acting on the advice of their tax accountant not to make another sale? Had they actually arrived at the street where the appointment was scheduled and determined, for some reason, that the neighborhood didn't fit their profile of a place where anyone would purchase their product? Or had they, for some reason, determined that they wouldn't make the sale anyway, so why bother going?

I suspect the last was the major reason they didn't show for the appointment. I believe they determined, for whatever reason, they wouldn't make the sale anyway so they didn't bother to show up. They were sure they would hear "No," so, in an effort to save precious time, they didn't bother to show up. Now this is a classic case of "stinking thinking."

Your mind is like a computer that you program. If you program your mind to believe a sale won't be made, why ask? Because you won't ask, you won't get the order. On the other hand, if you program your mind (your computer) with a positive thought, you will get the order, the prospect will buy, your mind will believe that program and expect to get the order. Your positive thinking will be subliminally transmitted to the prospect, and not only will you confidently ask for the order, your prospect more likely will feel that the decision to buy makes sense.

In the survey, of the six who did show for the appointment, only one on average asked the prospect to buy. Only one asked the prospect to make a buying decision. The other five simply left behind a price quotation or, worse, offered to mail the quote, without even asking the simplest of closing questions, "So, what do you think?"

You can't make a sale unless you ask for the order. Sure, a small percentage of people will take that action away from you, asking you how soon they can get it or where do they sign. However, by and large, if you're to get the order, you'll have to ask for it.

It's just that simple. When completing your presentation, ask the prospect a simple closing question. "Jack and Mary, the product completely installed is only $__, are mornings or afternoons more convenient for your installation?" And then shut up. The next one that speaks buys. That's simple isn't it?

So, why don't salespeople ask for the order? What stops them? Many salespeople fear they will hear the word *no*. They fear rejection. Some salespeople are so convinced the prospect won't make a buying decision, they simply don't ask. That's called *stinking thinking*. And stinking thinking surely will kill sales and, eventually, sales careers.

Don't decide in advance what the prospect might say. Have the courage to ask for the order. You'll be pleasantly surprised with the results. Next, you must understand and believe that the prospect who says "no" means "know"—"I don't know why I should say yes. I'm not convinced yet. Convince me."

One day, when I was driving a rental car en route to do a seminar, I heard a radio commercial that really makes the point.

A man was telling a woman, "Won't it be nice to drive down the street in this nice new car?" To which the woman replied, "Yes, it would be nice, but my old car still runs well and this is a lot of money." To which the man said, "Sure it is, but just picture yourself driving down the street with the top down and the wind blowing through your hair." And she said, "Wow that would be nice, but I can barely afford the payments I'm making on my old car." To which he countered, "But over 60 months, the payment for this brand new car probably will be less than what you're paying now, actually saving you money while you enjoy the benefits of this brand new convertible." There was a pause, then the woman said, "You're right, honey, let's go find a salesperson."

You see, the whole time I was listening to the commercial, I assumed, as you probably did, that this was a salesperson trying to sell the woman a car, not a husband convincing his wife to buy. We do this all the time. We often say "no" and don't really mean it. We say "no" and mean "know"—"Tell me why I should say yes. Convince me. I want to buy, just give me a nudge in that direction."

Some salespeople don't ask for the order because they fear being perceived as pushy. They don't want to be considered a pushy salesperson. However, there is a fine line between persistent and pushy, between convincing and pushy. It takes training and lots of practice to develop the skill to close without being pushy, and the steps of the close you will learn in a moment will help you achieve that objective.

I want to make one last point on asking for the order. When I started in sales over 30 years ago, my very first trainer said something to me that is as true today as it was then. He said to break down all the people in the United States into ratings of 1–10, in ranks of sales resistance. Persons in rating 1 will buy anything you try to sell them if only you ask. These people don't know how to say "No." All you have to do is ask them to buy.

Those in rating 10 won't buy anything from anyone. They wouldn't buy a $1000 bill for $10 if you tried to sell it to them.

Everyone else, the sales trainer said, falls somewhere between 1 and 10. To be successful in selling, he said, all you have to do is ask enough people to buy; odds are you'll find those rated 1, 2, 3, and 4, who will buy. All you have to do is ask. As a starting salesperson, that gave me a lot of comfort, as it should to you.

Asking for the order is and should be handled as the natural consummation of a high-quality, well-rehearsed presentation. By asking for the order, you are not being pushy or obnoxious. The prospect expects you to ask for the order. So don't disappoint him or her: Ask and you shall receive.

What if the prospect says, "No"? What then? How should you proceed? First, I recommend you learn the eight step closing pattern. The eight step close is designed to handle objections in a conversational manner rather than a confrontational manner. Instead of appearing to fight with prospects, you simply are agreeing with their feelings and turning the objection into a close.

Before we discuss answering objections, let's discuss the type objections you, as a security professional, encounter on a regular basis. The number 1 objection heard in all sales is, "I want to think it over. I want to sleep on it. We never make decisions on the first night."

The challenge with this objection is the absence of truth. Usually, when someone says he or she wants to think it over, that person is hiding the real reason from you. The prospect simply is telling you what he or she thinks will get rid of you. So let's evaluate what may be the truth in this situation. I believe there are three possibilities when people say they want to think it over.

First, they may want some time to think. They actually may need some time to mull it over. Now, I'm sure some of you sales pros are now saying, "What's Lou talking about? Is he suggesting we give the prospect time to think it over? Doesn't Lou know sales are lost that way?" Have patience with me; you'll soon see where I'm going with this.

Of course you're right. However, in a small percentage of situations I believe the prospect wants just a little time to talk it over with the spouse—and do so without you, the salesperson, staring at them. They would like to talk in private. So, ask yourself this question: "How much time do they need?" When I ask this question at seminars, the answers I get range from overnight, to a couple of days, to over the weekend, to a week or so. The average answer is a couple of days. I believe a couple of minutes is more like it. A few minutes for the husbands and wives to look at each other and say, "What do you think, honey?" That's it, five minutes tops.

I don't believe for one minute that the prospects actually will think about it or discuss it over days and weeks. And the prospects who say they like to sleep on it can't really mean what they're saying. I get this mental picture of the prospect writing on his bed before going to sleep, taking my proposal and placing it under the sheets before going to sleep. Does your prospect want to make an important decision when he or she is unconscious? I don't think so.

So, why not give them five minutes to think it over. That's all most people need. In most cases, the prospects didn't know all the details of being protected by a security alarm system. They didn't know how much the monthly investment would be. And, perhaps, they just want to look at each other and ask the simple questions, "What do you think, honey? Can we squeeze this amount into our monthly budget? What can we give up to enjoy this product?"

Sometimes, the couple made an agreement between each other before you arrived. They agreed they wouldn't buy anything today. They agreed to wait and think about it. Sometimes the wife made the appointment with you, and the husband, on finding out, told her he's not interested. He agreed to sit for the appointment because his wife already made it, but he told her before you arrived he's not buying. However, after hearing your presentation, he changed his mind. He saw the value of the product or service. Now he needs to tell his wife to forget what he said before your arrival. Let me give you an example of what I mean.

Several years ago, when my youngest son Jason was a junior in high school, I was on the road doing sales seminars. Late in the week I received a voice mail message from my wife Debbie, who wanted to know the precise time I would be home on Friday. When I called her back, I asked why.

She explained that she had received a phone call from someone in the school system about Jason. The caller asked if we were interested in grant money for Jason's college education. She, of course, said "yes." "So," Debbie said, "I need to know what time you'll be home so we can meet with the person about this." In my home, Debbie pays all the bills. In fact, I don't even see my check, it is deposited directly. Because I travel so much, she makes most of the decisions in the home. She doesn't need me for that.

I reminded her of that and suggested she alone meet with the person. "Just take the money," I said. "They said we both have to meet with the person coming over," she said. Red lights started flashing in my mind. "We both have to be there? What is this person selling?" I asked Debbie. "Nothing," she said, "it's just grant money." You know and I knew, if we both had to be present for the appointment, someone was trying to sell something to us.

"Debbie," I said, "I guarantee this person will try to sell us insurance. And I have too much insurance now. I'm worth more dead than alive. I'm not buying any more." Debbie agreed, still convinced the person wasn't selling anything.

That Friday we sat in our living room listening to the representative's presentation. Sure enough, it was insurance. However, grant money was involved. The company knew how to get through the paper and bureaucracy maze to get grant money and would do it for those families it insured. Also a bit of interest-free loan was involved.

Now remember, before the appointment I told my wife I would not buy more insurance. However, as I listened, I became interested, I changed my mind. The whole time my wife listened, she probably was saying to herself, "He was right. It's insurance, and he's not interested." So, at the end of the presentation, I needed a couple of minutes to tell Debbie that in fact I was interested. Although I said I didn't want insurance, this sounded good. We needed the money for Jason's tuition, so I didn't mind buying a little more insurance. I needed a minute or so to tell Debbie that, and the sale would have been made.

What happened next will floor some of you professional salespeople. As predicted, Debbie told the salesperson we needed some time to think this over; translation, we're not buying. My head was in the process of turning toward my wife so I could tell her I was interested, when the salesperson committed an unforgivable sin, he asked if a couple of weeks would be enough time to think it over. We said, "Sure." We never bought the insurance, and we never got the grant money. And, of course, the salesperson didn't get the sale. Everybody lost.

When the prospect says he or she wants to think it over, why don't you say this—the five minute close: "You know, Jack and Mary, I can appreciate your wanting to take some time to think this over. After all, a decision as important as this certainly is worth thinking about. I have another appointment right after this one, and I'd like to call my office to check directions and verify the appointment address, that should take about five minutes. So why don't I just step into the other room and call my office. This will give you two time to discuss this between yourselves. Fair enough?"

You'll be surprised how many times the prospects will agree to this proposal. You'll be even more surprised how many times the answer you get after the five minute break will be, "Yes. When can we get started?" Had the insurance salesman said that to us instead of suggesting two weeks, we would have bought the policy five minutes later. Instead, he got nothing. Have the courage to do this, and you'll succeed more than you'll fail.

Next, some people say they want to think it over and don't really know why they said it. They really don't want to think your proposal over, they're saying they want to think it over out of pure habit. They always say that. Their parents did also, and they learned from them. Which reminds me of a story that really makes this point.

One day a couple, Jim and Carla, went to a reunion, barbecue, and cookout at a family member's home. As is usually the custom, each couple would prepare part of the meal. This time Carla's job was to prepare the ham. Carla had a reputation for fixing delicious hams.

Carla was in the kitchen when Jim walked in. Jim noticed that Carla chopped off one end of the ham, turned it around, and then chopped off the other end. This prompted Jim to ask, "Why did you do that? Why did you cut the ends off the ham? Is it because the meat is sweeter in the center? Or is it because the meat is fattier on the ends?" Carla thought about the question for a moment and said, "Well, I don't know exactly. My mother always cut the ends off and I guess that's why I do. However, I'm sure," she continued, "it's for a good reason."

After Carla put the ham in the oven, she walked into the living room where her mother was sitting and asked, "Mom, why do you cut the ends off a ham before baking it? Jim saw me do it and asked me why, and frankly, I don't know why." Everyone was now looking at Carla's mother. After some thought, she said, "You know, Carla, I don't know. I think it's because Grandma always did and I learned to cook from her." Well, now the mystery was getting deeper. Jim, Carla, Carla's mother, and several of her relatives who heard Carla's question followed Carla's mother into the yard in search of Grandma.

The whole entourage found Grandma sitting on a lawn chair.

Carla's mother explained the situation. She explained about what Jim had asked Carla and then Carla asked her; now we all need to ask you, "Why did you cut both ends off the ham before you cooked it?" Grandma looked at everyone like they were nuts and said, "Because I had a pan only this big, the whole ham didn't fit the baking pan."

Forgive me. I know it's a long story to make a point, but it makes the point as well as anything I've ever heard.

Some people say they want to think it over and don't know why. Some people always "sleep" on decisions and haven't a clue why they do it. If they asked Mom and Dad, Grandma and Grandpa, they'd probably find it's because of a lifelong habit. People generally don't trust their own ability to make good decisions. Putting off a decision is safer.

The third, and most prevalent, reason people say they want to think it over is because they don't want to tell you the truth. They don't want to tell you what they're really thinking, so they lie instead. Don't get me wrong. I'm not saying buyers are liars. I'm not saying prospects will lie to you because they are liars. I believe prospects often lie to you to protect your feelings. They don't want to be cruel. If they don't believe your product is worth what you're asking for it, it's hard for them to say that to you. It's easier to say, "I want to think it over, we always sleep on decisions like this. We're in no particular hurry." However, you and I would rather have the prospect tell us the truth, rather than lie. We may be able to solve the problem if we know what it is.

To give you a real life example of how this works, let me tell you about the last time I lied to a salesperson trying to sell to me. A few years ago my company transferred me to the Minneapolis–St. Paul area of the country. I bought a home in Prescott, Wisconsin, right across the river from St. Paul. When I told my wife we were being transferred there, she asked for a couple of concessions to make the move more palatable. Because we were going to be empty nesters for the very first time, no children living at home, she wanted a couple of things. First, she wanted to replace some of the old furniture we acquired over the 20 plus years of raising a family; and second, she wanted nice landscaping at the new home. We never had a professionally landscaped home, and we always admired the houses that were nicely landscaped.

That was our plan. We found a fixer upper in Prescott, Wisconsin, had it renovated, bought the new furniture we planned on, and now it was time for the landscaping. Soon after we arrived in Prescott, we met many of the neighbors. When we noticed they had especially nice landscaping, we asked who they used. It didn't take long to realize that there was only one company to call. Everyone used it, and everyone was pleased with the work it did.

Before we called the landscaper, we sort of decided between us that landscaping should cost somewhere around $4000 or $5000. I don't know how we arrived at that amount, we just did. We were in agreement. So, Debbie called for an appointment. As luck would have it, the landscape representative, Gail, made an appointment to visit us at a time when I was home. When we met with her, she asked a lot of questions, trying to determine what we liked and what we were looking for. She asked if we had any plant preferences, did we want annuals or perennials or both. What about trees? She did a thorough job of determining what we liked. When she was finished with the survey, she explained the next step was for her to go back to the office and, over the next week or two, do some drawings to come up with a design or two she could present to us.

A week or so later, Gail called to schedule the second visit. When she came out the second time, she had two portfolios, two pedestals, and a briefcase. It took her two trips to get everything into my home. Then, she proceeded to make her presentation. And, I want to tell you, she blew me away. One after the other, she showed hand-drawn pictures of our home as it would look landscaped. She showed us how it would look in early spring, then how it would look in summer and fall. The landscaping was beautiful. She even figured in a small recirculating brook that flowed over rocks and spun a wooden wheel as it went by. It was gorgeous. We both were impressed and happy with what we saw; that is until she told us how much this beautiful plan would cost.

Now remember, Debbie and I agreed the landscaping would cost approximately $4000 or $5000, not chicken feed as far as we were concerned.

Now it was time. Gail was at the end of her presentation. She did a terrific job of selling us on her professionalism, the professionalism of her company, and the quality of her work. She did a wonderful job of showing us why everyone in our area selected her company, even though they had other choices. Everyone loved Gail's company, so we should, too. The whole job, Gail explained, could be completed for only $28,735—$28,735.

Then, I launched into the biggest series of lies you ever heard. And what impressed me was how Debbie was right there with me, lying through her teeth. I said "That's great, it's really beautiful, however, we hadn't planned to do anything right this minute. We always discuss things like this before do anything." Debbie chimed in, "That's right, and winter is coming and after all, we just finished the renovation. We'll probably wait until next spring to do something like this." And I jumped in full agreement. We were a team.

Gail's response to all this was, "Great! Shall I give you a call toward the end of winter?"

"No," I said, "we'll call you." It took us less than five minutes to get Gail out of the house. It took her two trips to get all her stuff into our home and it took us one to get it out. We carried most of it. We were great prospects. We liked Gail, and she liked us. As she drove out of our driveway, Debbie and I waved goodbye. When she was out of earshot, I looked at Debbie and said, "What is she nuts or something? I wanted to buy some plants not the entire nursery—$28,735, she's got to be out of her mind."

Guess what? I bet when Gail went into her office the next day and her manager asked her how it went last night with the Sepulvedas, she said, "Great! They really liked the plan. They're going to buy!" And I bet she put our name on her sales pending list. I bet she and her manager have reviewed her sales pending list several time since then, perhaps even giving each one a percentage possibility of closing. I bet my name is still on the list—and I've moved twice since then.

The truth is Gail had no chance of selling my wife and me. She had no chance because she bought our lies. She believed we wanted to discuss it. She believed we would buy later. The truth was we felt her price was much too high, and saying we wanted to think it over was an easy way for us to get rid of her without telling her what really was bothering us.

Had Gail been a true professional salesperson, she wouldn't have accepted my lie. She would have explored what I wanted to think about. If she approached it correctly, she would have discovered my real concern and probably would have made a sale, not one for $28,735 but a sale nonetheless. Instead, she got nothing but promises and Debbie and I didn't get the landscaping we wanted. Nobody won.

The next most common objection in sales is that the price is too high. Whether your installation fee or the monthly fee or both, it's too high. The question is, Too high as compared to what? As compared to the perceived value? As compared to another quote? As compared to what a neighbor paid? As compared to what?

No one wants to pay too much for anything. We all expect to pay a fair price. The challenge in selling alarm systems is that the prospect knows very little about what an alarm system should sell for. Therefore, we must be sure to build value into our presentation. And we must be prepared to handle and then overcome a price objection.

Another very common objection in sales is, "We plan to shop around." Ask yourself why? Why do people want to shop around? Do they truly want to spend an hour or so with several more salespeople? Do they really have that much time on their hands to spare? Are they really interested in having several more people, strangers, spend time in their homes? Obviously, the answer is no.

However, they will do exactly that because they want to be sure they're making a good decision. They want to be sure your product is the best for their needs. They don't want to be wrong. Fear is stopping them.

They also want to be sure they can believe you and trust you. That's really what it all breaks down to—trust. If they believed you and trusted you, they'd have no reason to shop. They would save a lot of time and just say yes. So, in sales, we must build trust if we're to expect the prospect to buy. See the puppy dog close explained later in this chapter.

Most people don't purchase a product or service because they truly believe they don't need it. They haven't experienced the need so far, so why buy one. However, anyone who has spent any time in the security industry knows better. We have met prospects who lived in the same home or the same neighborhood for many years who were burglarized for the first time. All it takes is one time and their peace of mind is shattered. They no longer feel safe in their own homes.

I've met people who said they are moving from the home they love, the neighborhood they love, because they were burglarized just once. I've met people who say their young children are so frightened since being burglarized they want to sleep with Mom and Dad again, something they haven't felt the need to do for many years.

Everyone needs a security system. And the security salesperson's job is to convince them of it. Therefore, it is obvious that we must build need into our presentations and be prepared to overcome the "I don't need one" objection.

Next, some people don't believe they need an alarm system because they have good insurance, replacement insurance. In some cases, they're so comfortable with this idea they'll say something like this to you: "I wish someone would burglarize my home and take some of this old stuff we have. If they take the TV, we'll get a newer, better one. If they take our computer, we'll get the newer version."

Obviously, insurance doesn't replace a life. It doesn't replace the peace of mind lost in a burglary. It doesn't replace the keepsakes lost in a fire. Think about the last time you saw a news report on TV about a home or town destroyed by a fire, hurricane, or tornado. When they show the victims going back to the remains of their homes, what are they looking for? What seems to be most important to them? The answer is pictures of the children growing up, irreplaceable treasures such as the china that belonged to their great grandmother, items that the best insurance in the world cannot replace. Once again, we must be prepared to handle this objection.

High on the list of objections that keep a family from protecting itself with an alarm system is the family dog. They feel their dog is all they need. We know this isn't true. Ask yourself this question: "What is the relationship between a dog and it's owners, the family?" If you answered a family member, you are correct. Many people refer to themselves as the dog's mommy or daddy. The dog is like one of the family. The relationship between dogs and families is an emotional issue. Emotionally, people feel protected by their dog. They do so even if it isn't logical to feel that way. Remember, when logic comes in conflict with emotions, emotions always win.

I have met prospects who were buying an alarm system for the first time because the family dog died. When I have asked about how the dog died, I have heard answers like the dog died of old age. People have explained that the dog was so old, he spent more time at the vet than at home, so old they had to force feed him. If that's true, what good was the dog as the family protector? None at all, right? However, as long as it was alive, they felt protected. This is emotional, not at all rational.

We also know dogs can and will be harmed by the burglar. We know that the family will grieve the loss of its dog. So we must build protecting pets into our presentation. We must put the family pet where it belongs, as a family member, one that needs protection along with the rest of the family.

Review the needs analysis in Chapter 11. Notice how I inquire about the family pet and its habits. The questions were designed to help me put the dog where it belongs, as a pet, a family member.

A discussion of objections isn't complete without talking about the person who feels owning a gun is all that's necessary: Jerry, the gun owner. You've met him. His ego says he's all the protection his family needs. He almost looks forward to the opportunity to prove his manhood by stopping a burglar with a bullet.

However, truth be known, when actually in the situation, who knows what he might do. I have met police officers, whose job it is to use a gun in the line of duty, requiring hours and months of therapy after having shot someone for the first time. It's not easy to shoot and kill someone. However, using logic on Jerry rarely works. Explaining the odds of a gun being used against you doesn't work with him. It won't happen to him. So, to handle this objection, you must be able to do so without challenging his fragile ego (see the "I have a gun" close later in this chapter).

Some object to buying a security system because they feel they have nothing to steal. Why would anyone break into my home, they wonder? Of course, the first fallacy here is they assume the burglar knows what they have or don't have. The fact is that burglars burglarize homes somewhat at random. The drug-influenced burglar will burglarize any home, because every home has something that can be fenced and converted into money to buy drugs. Burglars are not looking for the crown jewels. You know as do I that everyone is a potential crime victim. The proof is aired every day on TV. You've heard of burglars burglarizing empty, boarded-up homes, haven't you? What do they steal? No valuables are there. How broke can you get?

Well, there are valuables even in empty, boarded-up houses. They steal the doors, the flooring, old light fixtures, copper plumbing pipes, old tubs, and toilets. In one house I know of, they stole the stair railings along with everything else I mentioned. You see, all this stuff converts into cash, which buys drugs. The prospects who believe they won't be victims because they have nothing to steal are kidding themselves. It's our job to open their eyes before a burglar does.

And then there is the objection that the neighbors watch out for them or someone always is home. The person who objects in this manner is thinking the only reason to have a burglar alarm system is to prevent loss of possessions. This person hasn't considered the more important function of an alarm system, protection of life. If someone is always home, I believe they need an alarm system even more.

If you're to be successful in this business, you must develop a presentation that opens the prospect's eyes to the dangers an alarm system is designed to protect against. When you do that, you may never encounter this objection (see the steps to successful selling in Chapter 11).

Now that we have a better feeling for the objections we may encounter and, as important, why people feel as they do, it becomes your responsibility to learn and practice answers to the common objections. For when you do, two important things happen. First, you'll make more sales, more money, and solidify your career. Second, and very important, you'll leave happy customers and families in your wake.

After 28 years of selling and protecting people with alarm systems, I can honestly say I've never known or met anyone who was sorry to have invested in a security system. On the contrary, I have met numerous people whose lives were saved by the system I sold them and many more whose lives were made safer and happier as a result of the system I convinced them to buy. I sleep well at night with that knowledge, and so will you, if you'll read this chapter over and over until you internalize the answers and the words become yours.

CLOSING PATTERN

As mentioned before, the eight step close is designed to handle objections in a conversational manner rather than a confrontational manner. Instead of appearing to be fighting with prospects, you are simply agreeing with their feelings and turning their objection into a close.

While it is easy to use shortcuts in the process of closing, following the eight steps assures a more friendly feel to the whole process, making the result—the sale of the product—more achievable. So let's review the eight step closing pattern.

Step 1. Listen

The first step of the closing pattern is to listen. I know this seems obvious. Of course, we have to listen. But the fact of the matter is, we as salespeople often don't listen as well as we should. We tend to pick up on the first few words out of the prospect's mouth and assume we know what else he or she plans to say. The problem is that we may be wrong. Prospects may want to correct what they said. They may want to cancel what they said, as not having merit. They may want to add to what they said. If all we hear are the first few words, we'll miss the rest, and subsequently answer the wrong objection.

Have you ever thought of something you wanted to say; however, when the words came out of your mouth, you determined the words didn't completely express your true thoughts, so you had to restate your words, your feelings? We all have experienced this. So when we listen completely and intently to the words the prospect is using, we avoid the danger of missing valuable data. We avoid the risk of answering the wrong objection.

To listen effectively, avoid thinking. Avoid thinking because, when you're thinking, you're not listening. The prospect's words become a blur of sound, completely unintelligible. Focus on what the prospect is saying and what the prospect means by that. When you listen intently to the prospect, you may hear words that contradict the objection he or she is giving you. You may hear the truth.

Step 2. Pause

While looking directly into the eyes of the prospect, don't say a word. Think of what you might say in response to what the prospect said. You weren't allowed to think while the prospect was talking, so now is the time to think. If, while you are thinking and looking into the prospect's eyes, you see his or her mouth begin to move again, stop thinking and begin listening again. You may find the objection has changed or, at the very least, the prospect may give you more information. The pause step can be the most subtle pressure you can use in a close. Prospects may talk themselves into buying with little to no encouragement from you.

Step 3. Empathize

This is an extremely important step because empathy assures prospects you understand their feelings. This is where they expect you to argue with them. Instead, you agree with them, you demonstrate you understand them. Showing and expressing empathy relaxes prospects. It makes them more willing to see your point of view. To be successful you should know at least two empathy statements for each type of objection you may hear.

Step 4. Repeat but Change the Objection

Sometimes, when hearing the objection, the prospect finds he or she no longer can agree with it, no longer can buy it. Sometimes, when hearing the objection repeated, the prospect changes the objection to one that better describes his or her feelings. This, of course, is good for you, it serves no purpose to answer an objection that is not the valid one. The "but change" part of this step is new and very effective. You change the objection by adding words you would've rather heard as part of the objection. Wouldn't you rather hear the prospect object in this manner: "I really like your product or service and would purchase it as soon as possible but . . . [the objection repeated]?"

I have never experienced a situation where the prospect said, "I didn't say I really like it and would get it as soon as possible. That's not what I said." Prospects always agree and say, "Yeah, that's about it." The repeat but change step is extremely effective and, when used properly, will bring you closer to a yes decision.

Step 5. Isolate the Objection

Before you answer an objection it is important you uncover all the roadblocks to getting the sale. If you don't, while you're busy answering the objection, the prospect could be thinking up new ones for you to answer.

This step also commits the prospect to his or her own objection. It has the person agree that this is the stumbling block; therefore, if you solve the problem, the obvious next step is to buy. Now that I know what is stopping the prospect from making a positive decision, I can proceed.

Step 6. Answer the Objection

Answer the objection with a verbal, written, or third party answer—or any combination of the three. A *verbal answer* is an answer you have memorized that handles a particular type of objection. Verbal answers can be serious in nature or can utilize humor to make a point. A *written answer* combines both verbal and written support. A *third party answer* references someone else, someone like them, who had a similar concern, but subsequently purchased the alarm system and now is happy.

After having been in the security alarm business for a year or more, a company most likely will have a customer who, at first, didn't buy the security system someone tried to sell him or her. The prospect put off the decision in favor of something else felt to hold a higher priority, such as furniture for a new home, draperies, replacing a car, or household appliances. Subsequently, however, this person was burglarized and afterward bought an alarm system. Obviously, given hindsight, the person would've purchased the alarm system before the burglary. The purchase of an alarm system would've held a much higher priority.

Get a letter from that customer, explaining what happened and what the person wished he or she would have done. This is one of the best third party answer tools you could ever want. When prospects say they want to think over the decision, you can reference this letter. If prospects say they have a higher priority item to spend their money on, you can reference the third party customer letter.

Step 7. Qualify Your Answer

The qualifying step is simply a tag line at the end of the answer, such as "That makes sense, doesn't it; solves the problem, doesn't it?"

Step 8. Ask for the Order

Step 8 takes you right back to where you started. Please don't forget this step. This is the whole reason you are there. Nothing happens until a sale is made.

9

Answers to Common Objections

You have heard how to handle common objections using the eight step closing pattern. Now let's discuss answers to objections you may encounter in selling.

> Objection: I Want to Think It Over
> Answer: The Five Minute Close

> The Sales Pro: You know, Jack and Mary, I can appreciate your wanting to take some time to think this over. After all, a decision as important as protecting your family from fire and crime certainly is worth thinking about. I have another appointment right after this one, and I'd like to call my office to check directions and verify the appointment address, that should take about five minutes. So why don't I just step into the other room and call my office. This will give you two time to discuss this between yourselves. Fair enough?

You'll be surprised how many times they'll say yes to this proposal. And you'll be even more surprised how many times the answer they give you after the five minute break will be, "Yes. When can we get it installed." Had the insurance salesman said that to us instead of suggesting two weeks, we would have bought the policy five minutes later. Instead he got nothing. Have the courage to do this and you'll succeed more than you'll fail.

> Objection: I Still Want to Think It Over
> Answer: The "Is It?" Close

Here's how the salesperson should have handled the situation. When my wife and I said we wanted to think it over, she should have said the following.

> The Sales Pro: You know, Lou and Debbie, I can completely understand how you feel. After all, landscaping your beautifully renovated home is an important decision, one that shouldn't be made hastily. However, let's see if I can help you. When you say you want to think about it, is it me as your landscape designer you want to think about? I hope I've done all you wanted me to do for you?

We would have said, "No, you've done a great job." And she did.

> The Sales Pro: Then, since it's not me you have to think over, is it my company you want to consider? We take great pride in our company. In fact, we've done most of the nice landscaping jobs in your area. Is it my company you want to think about?

To which we would have replied, "No, your company has a great reputation. We talked to the neighbors already."

The Sales Pro: So you don't have to think about my company. Are you happy with the design I came up with? Is that what you want to think over?

We would have said, "No, your design is beautiful, we love it."

The Sales Pro: So it's not the design you have to consider, how about the plants we selected, did you like them?

We would have said we loved the plants.

The Sales Pro: Well then, all that's left is the investment. Could it be the money you're considering?

To which we would have said, "It is more than we figured on spending."

The Sales Pro: When you say it's more than you figured on spending, how much too much is it?

Given that we expected the project to cost $4000—5000 (and given we had no clue why we thought it would cost that), I would have said something like this: "We were thinking it would be in the neighborhood of $9,000—10,000; $28,000 is just more than we want to invest at this time." Now the truth is out. No longer is a think it over the issue. It's price.

Armed with that information, we can now approach the situation from a couple of angles. First, we can find the parts of the project the prospect can live without for a while. When we explore those possibilities, two things will happen. The landscaper will eliminate unimportant aspects of the design, and we will raise our own investment to accommodate the parts of the design we want. We do the same in a burglar alarm sale to find the true objection, most often price, and then solve it.

The next most common objection in sales is that the price is too high. Whether it is the installation fee or the monthly fee or both, it's too much. The question is, Too high as compared to what: their perceived value, another quote they received, what a neighbor paid?

No one wants to pay too much for anything. We all expect to pay a fair price. The challenge in selling is that the prospect usually knows very little about what your product should sell for. Therefore, we must be sure to build value into the presentation. And we must be prepared to overcome a price objection.

Objection: The Price Is Too High
Answer: The Reduce to the Ridiculous Close

Let's assume the investment figure you quoted for an alarm system was $850 plus monitoring. And let's suppose the prospects figured it would cost approximately $350 plus monitoring. Here's how to handle the objection.

The Sales Pro: So, Sam and Gloria, now that we know the challenge we face with this decision, let's see if we can find a solution. You say you were expecting the system to come in around $350, instead of the $850 figure I presented, is that correct?

Sam and Gloria: Yes.

The Sales Pro: That represents a difference of approximately $500. Let's see what we can do about that.

The Sales Pro (continuing): Considering the quality of the product and the reputation of our company, would you agree a system like this should last in your home for at least 10 years, do you think that's fair?

Gloria: I would hope so.

The Sales Pro: Sure it should. It should last at least 10 years, so over the 10 year time frame, that equals a difference of $50 per year. Which represents approximately $4 per month, approximately $1 per week. That equals only 14 cents per day. Sam and Gloria, doesn't it make sense for you to protect your loved ones and precious belongings with the absolute best for the difference of only 14 cents per day, almost half the price of a phone call?

Sam: Yes.

The Sales Pro: So when would it be convenient to install your system, Tuesday or Friday?

Isn't that a great way to find the real objection and then put the difference into its proper perspective?

Objection: We Don't Need an Alarm System
Answer: Overcoming the Psychological Law of Self-
    Exception

Ask yourself this question: What percentage of your town's population doesn't need an alarm system. Who doesn't need one? When I ask this question of salespeople who have been in the alarm business for over six months the answer I always hear is that everyone needs an alarm system. However, over 80 percent of the people think they don't need an alarm system. This is obvious because they don't have one. However, if they get burglarized tonight, all of a sudden they will know they need one.

Why do you think that is? Why do people think they do not need an alarm system?

The answer is the psychological law of self-exception.

The psychological law of self-exception says that I'm not going to have a problem: My home won't be burglarized, my home won't catch fire. There is no logical reason why I can say that, but I prefer to believe it is so. That is why smokers continue to smoke. People who are dangerously overweight don't diet. Youngsters and adults use heroin or crack or other highly addictive drugs in spite of the obvious danger such use exposes them to. It doesn't matter how much evidence is produced to establish the danger. The psychological law of self-exception allows me to believe that it won't happen to me.

People truly believe they don't need an alarm system because they've never had a burglary. They believe they have nothing to steal, at least nothing a burglar is going to break into their house for. As I mentioned earlier, burglars break into empty, boarded-up houses. They steal doors, door frames, stair railings, and copper from the pipes and air conditioners. They steal flooring material, old toilets, and other plumbing fixtures. Give them enough time, they'll steal the entire house. Nothing will be left but the lot. Then they'll steal the dirt, for fill. A burglar will steal anything that can be sold. So, how can anyone legitimately say he or she has nothing to steal? They can't, you and I know that. The trouble is our prospects don't know. That is why they honestly may say they don't need the system. But it doesn't mean it's true.

The insurance close is an effective close to handle "no need." An alarm system is much like an insurance policy. You buy one because you should, not because you really want one. And, you hope you'll never have to use it.

Objection: We've Never Had a Problem, We Live in a
   Safe Neighborhood
Answer: The Insurance Close

The insurance close is an extremely effective way to handle the objection "I don't think I need a system," as well as the one that says, "I already have insurance." After hearing the objection, you say this to the prospect.

The Sales Pro: I can understand your feelings, you don't want to invest money into something you feel you have no need for—that makes sense. However, let me see if I completely understand you. You're saying that you like the system and you would install it as soon as possible if you thought you needed it, is that correct?
Prospect: Yes.

The Sales Pro: Other than need, does anything else prevent you from saying, "Let's protect my family right away?"

The Prospect: No, I just don't feel we need one.

The Sales Pro: How long have you lived in this home?

The Prospect: Five years.

The Sales Pro: How long do you plan to live here?

The Prospect: At least another 10 years.

The Sales Pro: I see, so altogether, if your plans don't change, you will have lived in this home for a total of 15 years. Do you recall how much you invest in homeowners' insurance per year?

The Prospect: Approximately $450.

The Sales Pro: Let me draw a picture of your home, and then draw a line down the middle, like this.

The Sales Pro: As I see it, you are investing $450 per year times 15 years, which equals $6750 to protect half of your home; that is, your furniture, fixtures, rugs, ceiling, roof, and replaceable items. And that's a good investment. What I'm suggesting is that you invest $850 to protect the other half of your home, the most important

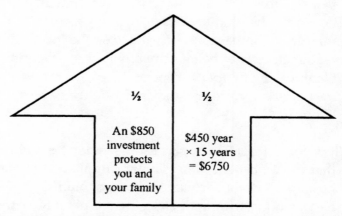

Fig. 9.1 Homeowner's Insurance vs. Security Protection

half of your home—you, your spouse, your children and pets, and irreplaceable possessions—that makes sense doesn't it?

The Prospect: Yes.

The Sales Pro: So, would a morning or afternoon installation work best for you?

Objection: We Need Time to Consider This
Answer: The Ben Franklin Close

The Ben Franklin close is one of the oldest but still one of the most effective closes to handle the think about it objection as well as the shop around objection. The Ben Franklin close uses logic to support the emotional reason to buy. The Ben Franklin close goes like this.

The Sales Pro: You know, Jack and Mary, when my wife and I are faced with a difficult decision to make, we often take a page from Ben Franklin's book, where he explains how he made decisions. You may be aware that Ben Franklin was known to be an excellent decision maker. Well, one day some of Ben's associates approached him and asked how he so consistently made good decisions. Ben said this: "When I'm faced with a difficult decision, I take out a blank piece of paper. I draw a line down the middle of the page, and then across the top. (While explaining the lines being drawn, you draw the same on a blank piece of paper for them.) Then, on the left side of the page Ben wrote *Yes*, and on the right side he wrote *No*. (Do it.)

After doing that, Ben began listing under *Yes* the reasons that would benefit him. Having completed the *Yes* side, he began listing the reasons why he should say *No*. When he was done with both sides, he simply added the reasons for each and the side that was greater usually was the better decision.

Why don't we try Ben's method with the decision you face today. Let's start with the reasons why you would benefit from the installation of our security system.

You should, of course, be prepared to help with the *Yes* decisions. But do not help with the *No* decisions. Once the *Yes* and *No* answers are on the paper, add up each side and then say this.

> The Sales Pro: It appears we have found 10 reasons why you would benefit by owning a high-quality security system and only 2 reasons against the decision. Ben Franklin would say our decision is quite clear. So, when is a good time for installation? Would you rather schedule a morning or afternoon appointment?

Key to this close is for you to have memorized 8–10 reasons your prospect would benefit from having a security burglar and fire alarm system installed, helping them with that part of the close.

> Objection: We Want to Think About It
> Answer: The Balance Scale Close

Let's review a new, very effective close that uses many of the elements of the Ben Franklin close. It's called the *balance scale close*.

When the prospect objects by saying he or she needs time to think it over, after listening then pausing, you say this.

> The Sales Pro: I can understand that. Are you saying you want time to weigh the facts?

The prospect normally will agree.

> The Sales Pro: You know, Jack and Mary, when faced with an important decision like this one, I like to weigh the facts, too. And I've found a method to do so that

is quite effective, let me show you how the method works.

First, I take a clean sheet of paper and on it I draw a scale, like the scale a jewelry store might use. Next, on the left side of the scale, I start listing the reasons why the decision I'm trying to make makes sense. I do so by drawing a small weight for each reason and placing it on the yes side of the scale.

When I'm finished with the yes side, I start on the no side with the reasons why I shouldn't go ahead. When done, the side with the most weights usually is the better decision. Why don't we give the weighing method a chance here. Let's list the first reason you would benefit by owning this product or service.

As with the Ben Franklin close, here is where you want to provide lots of help. Let the prospects answer for themselves; however, when they begin to run out of reasons and you know there are more, suggest reasons to them and get their agreement on each.

After you get 8 or 10 reasons to say yes, and if there are no more, ask for the reasons they wouldn't benefit by saying yes to the product or service. Usually, the prospects are hard-pressed to find more than two or three, most often they'll find only one, the price. When they are finished, you say this.

The Sales Pro: Well then, let's count the weights on the yes side of the scale. Let's see, we have 10 heavy reasons why we should go ahead and only 2 reasons why we shouldn't. Ten is far greater than two, so I guess our decision is made for us. Which day would be better for installation, Tuesday or Thursday?
(Then shut up. The next one that speaks buys.)

The balance scale close works so well because it is a logical way to make a decision. It is unemotional.

Objection: Your Price Is Too High
Answer: The Parachute Close

Let's suppose your prospect has seen or heard about another company's system whose monitoring charge is $21.95 versus your $29.95. You should say this.

> The Sales Pro: I can understand how you feel, no one wants to spend too much for anything. (This is the empathy step.)
> But let me see if I completely understand you, what you're saying is you really like the system and would have it installed as soon as possible, but you think it cost a bit too much, is that about right? (This is the repeat but change step.)
> Other than the monthly investment does anything prevent you from saying, "Hey, Lou, let's protect my family right away"? Is there anything else? (This is the isolate step.)
> So it's just the price difference? If we are able to solve that problem, we can get you protected? Is that right?
> The Prospect: Yes.
> The Sales Pro: Great! Help me out here, how much too much is it?

The prospect tells you how much.

> The Sales Pro: Let's see if I can make some sense of this for you. Let's pretend you won a raffle. You know how children will come to your door from time to time selling raffle tickets? Well let's suppose this time you bought one and received a call to say you had won. You won an all expense paid trip for two to Amsterdam. All expenses means they'll pay your airfare, your hotel, your meals, and even give you some cash to spend—truly a free trip. Wouldn't that be great?

Let's further suppose you made arrangements with work to take some vacation time and today is the day. Today you have arrived at La Guardia Airport in New York and boarded a 747 bound for Amsterdam.

If you have ever flown before, you know that when the plane gets to cruising altitude the pilot or copilot usually makes an announcement that the plane is approaching a cruising altitude of, let's say, 30,000 feet and if you look out the right side of the plane that is the Statue of Liberty and out the left side is the Empire State Building, like anyone can see anything from that height or cares to.

Well today the pilot comes on to make an announcement but, instead of the normal message, here's what you hear:

Ladies and gentleman, I have some bad news. For some unknown reason the four engines that power this 747 have failed. We have been trying desperately to get them started again to no avail. I'm afraid this aircraft is going to crash. Also, for some reason, the ground crew failed to place enough parachutes on this aircraft for our passengers, they did put enough on for us on the flight deck so—well—God bless!

Just about that time you look out the window and you see parachutes opening. This is not a pretty picture is it? Well just about the time you would all begin to panic— and I'm sure we all would—I jump up and say:

Ladies and gentleman, don't panic. I'm a parachute sales-person and I happen to have enough parachutes with me to accommodate all of you. I have two types. Mr. Jones, you're first in line, so you get first pick. You see I have one para-chute that will cost you $21.95 per month and is guaranteed to open most of the time. However, it does come with a money back guarantee, so if it doesn't open, when you hit the ground just bring it back to our office, well you probably wouldn't be able to . . . so just have someone else bring it back to our office and we'll give a 100 percent refund. Or you can choose the other type parachute, the best one made, which will cost you $29.95 and is guaranteed to open all of the time. Which parachute are you going to strap on your back when jumping from the plane?

The reply usually is, "Of course, the best one."

The Sales Pro: Of course, the $29.95 parachute. Because, when it comes to your life and the lives of your loved ones, cheap is not good enough. Only the best is good enough. You see, that's what we're talking about here. The lives of you and your family. When a burglary or fire happens you want only the very best. (This is a verbal answer.)
Isn't that so? (This is the qualifying statement.)
What would be more convenient for you, a morning or afternoon installation? (You ask for the order.)

Isn't that a great close? And, isn't it true? Sure it is. When it comes to living or possibly dying no one picks cheap. You get the best you can buy. The parachute close employs humor to make a serious point. An alarm system is a life safety device. It is not an appliance, where at the very worst you'll be inconvenienced if it doesn't work. Your life could ride on the decision. And, in that event, cheaper is not the answer.

Objection: I Plan to Shop Around
Answer: The Puppy Dog Close

If you had to rate objections by the frequency in which they are heard in selling, shop around falls somewhere between numbers 2 and 3. You have to ask yourself, Why? Why do people want to shop around? The answer is that they want to check whether a better deal is available. They want to check whether your product is as good as you say it is. They want to see if they can believe everything you've said. So it's a matter of trust and belief. If they trusted and believed you, they would have no need to shop. They would believe you when you said your product is the best. They would believe you when you said your price is the right price to pay for the product. But, because they don't trust you entirely or believe you entirely, they want to shop.

Well, why not just let them shop? You know your product is the best, and you know your price is fair for the products and service you're providing. So why not just leave and let them get their shopping over with? You must not do that.

Veteran salespeople have learned the hard way that, once you leave the house, once you let a day or two, a week or two, go by, the prospect forgets most of the valid reasons you presented to support the purchase of your system.

Worse yet, after seeing a couple of other companies, prospects no longer are sure who offered what. They begin to confuse features and benefits of your system with features and benefits of someone else's. They become more and more confused. Your systems and pricing are the best, and prospects couldn't do better, no matter how long or hard they looked. And as they take the time to look around, they remain unprotected.

So let's answer a shop around objection using one of the most powerful closes ever used (if you have the confidence to use it): Let's answer it with the puppy dog close.

The situation is this.

> The Sales Pro: Is the morning or afternoon better for an installation?
>
> The Prospect: We're not ready to make a decision right now, we planned to look at a couple of other companies before making a decision. (This is the objection.)
>
> The Sales Pro: (Pause, they may have more to say. Then empathize with the prospect.) I can understand that . . . after all, we all want to be sure of a decision we're making.
>
> But, let's see if I completely understand you. (Here you use the repeat but change.) What you're saying is you

really like the system and would have it installed as soon as possible, but you want to look at other companies to be sure ours is the best overall package. Is that about right?

So then other than looking around, is there anything else that would prevent you from saying, "Hey, Lou, let's protect my family right away." Anything else? (You isolate the objection.)

You know, Jack and Mary, I'm happy you're going to take the time to look at other companies. Even though I know you're going to invest several more hours of your valuable time—time that I'm sure you could use doing other important things—I'm happy, because I know that, the harder you look, the better my company will look to you.

After comparing what we have to offer—in product, monitoring, company stability, and reliability—I know you'll agree that my company is the best for your family. The only challenge I have with this is I don't have a crystal ball, as I'm sure you don't. If we did, we'd all win the lottery and probably wouldn't be sitting here talking about this. So I can't be sure—nor can you—that you won't have a problem, a burglary or a fire, during the time you're looking around. However, I have a solution for you. I'll send an installation crew over here tomorrow morning and we'll install a basic package of protection: your front door, back door, a motion detector, and smoke detector. That way, while you're looking at other companies,

1. You'll have the benefit of enjoying at least the basic protection package.
2. You'll be able to directly compare my system and monitoring services with the system and monitoring service other companies are recommending.

3. If, after you check out the other companies, you decide that some other company or product is better for you, all you have to do is call and we'll pull out the system we installed and you would have enjoyed the protection while you shopped absolutely free. Will two weeks be enough time for you to check out other companies? Great, so then we'll have our crew here in the morning.

Now let's evaluate what just happened.

1. Although there is no obligation on the part of the prospects to keep my system with the puppy dog close, will they feel obligated nonetheless? Yes, they will.
2. Aren't most of our prospects busy people, just like us? Then, is it possible that, even though they fully intended to get other quotations, inasmuch as there is a system working in their home, they may procrastinate in calling other companies and never call for a second quote? I think this is highly possible.
3. Now let's look at the quality of our competition. I said earlier in this book I had conducted a survey and, of 10 companies called for an alarm sales appointment, only 6 showed up. Further, of the six who showed, only one asked for the order. How strong are our competitors' salespeople? Is it possible that, after we install the puppy dog system and of course plant a new protected-by sign in the lawn, even if the prospects made additional appointments, the salesperson seeing the new yard sign would just leave, thinking the prospect already bought another system and just didn't bother to cancel the appointment?
4. If the salesperson didn't leave, when the customer opens the door, the alarm system I installed will go beep beep. What's the sales rep going to think? Is the rep's five day deodorant pad breaking down about

now? Is this person in the best of moods? Do you warm up people and sell well when you're mad?

The puppy dog close is a powerful close, and when used, you'll almost never take one out. After all, even if the customer found what he or she thinks is a better deal, you'll still have the last shot at debunking the better deal or the last shot to match it.

Objection: I Have a Gun and I Will Use It
Answer: The Early Warning System

You won't be in security alarm sales for long before meeting the prospect I like to call Jerry. Jerry has a gun and is quick to tell you how he'll use the gun on anyone stupid enough to burglarize his home. He'll "kill the B——!" Have you met this guy?

This person lives in every part of the United States and probably the world. Something you should know about this person is that logic doesn't work. Please don't try to use statistics. Don't tell him four out of five gun owners will have their own guns used against them. This one'll just say, "Not me. I'll kill the A——!"

Here is a way to work with Jerry's ego and make the sale. When faced with the gun objection, turn to the wife.

The Sales Pro (with a big smile): You know, Betty, you are a lucky lady! You're lucky because you have a husband like Jerry, who I'm convinced will protect you and your home should anyone be stupid enough to burglarize your home while he's here. He'd use the gun wouldn't he?
(She'll usually nod yes. Now, look at the husband.) Jerry, there are at least two reasons why you're going to love this system. First, this system will work like the best hunting dog you ever saw. If a burglar attempts to burglarize your home when you are at home, whether you

are awake or asleep, like a hunting dog, the system will alert you and tell you exactly from where the burglar is entering your home. This will give you the time to load your guns and be ready for him. Isn't that great?

Second, in the event you are not home to protect your family, the system will still be there to sound the alarm and summon police. And, of course, that is what you want, isn't it?

So, are mornings or afternoons better for you, Jerry?

By using this method, you are not challenging Jerry's fragile ego. You are not saying he is incapable of protecting his family. You are pointing out a feature of the system, zone reporting, that could be useful to him. All people like to be warned if someone is trying to attack them. And everyone would want to know where the attacker is coming from. Use this close and you'll handle and then protect Jerry's family more often than not.

I conduct dozens of sales seminars throughout the United States and Canada every year, and I always strongly emphasize the need to become a better closer. People who attend my seminars and know me, know I'm emotional about closing and selling skills.

The security alarm field is a "life safety" business. What we do can make the difference between life and death. Our systems can make the difference between families enjoying their homes or moving.

As professionals in sales, it always is important that we learn how to close the sale; however, in security sales our responsibility goes deeper. Our prospects' lives and well-being depend on our persuasive skills, not to mention our families and employers.

Learn and internalize the closing skills outlined in this chapter, and I guarantee your income and life will improve.

Let me leave you with this final thought about closing the sale: You owe it to your prospect to be the best salesperson you can be. You know your prospect needs this protection. You know there is no way you or I or the customer can be sure we won't be a victim of a burglary or fire. It's your job and it should be your personal mission to protect people from the twin perils of fire and crime. We sell "heartware" not hardware. This is a job and a personal mission you can live with.

10

Motivate the Troops

Once you've provided the initial training salespeople need to get started, motivating them to do the things they must do to be successful is critical. We all are motivated by something; however, the same things do not always motivate us personally. To help my salespeople succeed and at the same time help my company succeed, it is critical that I find out what motivates each salesperson individually. What are the individual's goals and aspirations? What would cause this person to stretch out, to reach out, and grab the gold ring?

Motivation falls into four basic categories: fear, praise and recognition, money, and personal satisfaction. Before I go further, let me acknowledge that there may be many other categories or subcategories, but in my estimation, these are the basic four.

The least effective motivation for salespeople is fear. Fear may motivate some classifications of workers, but in my opinion, fear has a negative effect in sales. Suffice it to say, I must find what motivates my salesperson and use that reason to motivate him or her. Here is an example.

When interviewing a salesperson, I always ask how much money this person made last year and how much money he or she would like to earn this year with my company. For example, say the sales applicant made $35,000 last year and said she would like to earn $45,000 this year. My question to the salesperson is, "If you earned $45,000 this year, which is $10,000 more than you earned last year, what would you do with the extra $10,000?"

I often get a fuzzy response such as, "I'd improve my lifestyle." My next question would be, "How specifically would you improve your lifestyle?" (I'm looking for a specific goal, not a fuzzy one.) Suppose the salesperson said she'd buy a newer car. I'd then ask, "What type of car? What year? What color?" Focusing on the exact car, I'd instruct the salesperson to acquire a brochure and price for the newer car and post it over her desk or work area to constantly remind her of her goal.

Next, I'd help her develop an action plan designed to reach the specific goal within the time frame she wished to achieve the goal. After completing the plan, we would review the plan together. We'd agree on the achievability of the plan. I would ask the salesperson to sign the goal plan and then manage her toward this goal.

A salesperson has a better chance of achieving when he or she

1. Has a specific goal,
2. Commits to himself or herself and me the intention to reach that goal,
3. Signs the commitment.

Now, we're striving for the salesperson's goal, not mine.

Goal setting for salespeople is extremely important because our minds function best when programmed to a specific goal. Once programmed, our mind is like a heat seeking missile, locked on course, refusing to be shaken off.

When we set goals for ourselves, we have something against which to measure progress, a reason to reward ourselves on achieving the goal. Most people perform better when they know where they are trying to get and are rewarded when they get there. It's important, therefore, to help the new salesperson set long-term goals than many intermediate goals that lead to the long-term goal. Goals are much easier to achieve when they're broken down into smaller, bite-size pieces.

After determining the goal, let's say a newer car, and when to achieve it and once we lay out a plan of how the salesperson can reasonably reach the goal, with intermediate measurements or short-term goals, it is the job of management to keep the salesperson focused on his or her goal. We must manage the salesperson to his or her goal rather than ours.

Periodically, and I think weekly is good, we should check the salesperson's progress toward the goal. Inspect what you expect. If the salesperson strays too far from the goal, it's time to have a private discussion about the goal and what will get the salesperson back on track. Ask the salesperson if he or she needs help. Ask what you can do to help this individual get back on target. After all, that's what you both want.

Don't forget pats on the back. All people perform better when they see their efforts are noticed and appreciated. When you measure each person's success against the goal you both decided on, it is much easier to sincerely congratulate the salesperson for his or her achievements. If, on the other hand, you measure success against the best salespeople in the office or against a number you would like to see all salespeople reach, you may never find the reason to recognize significant improvement within a salesperson. And the salesperson, feeling unappreciated, may never reach his or her full potential. We in management are quick to find fault, to point out failures and policy infractions. We, all too often, fail to recognize performance, achievement.

One nice spring Saturday, Debbie and I were walking around a path at our local park. As we did so, we passed three ladies walking toward us and overheard what one of them was saying to the other two. She said, "Mr. Jackson [not his real name] never thanks me or recognizes when I do something right, but let me do something wrong, and I never hear the end of it." We all want to know we're appreciated, regardless of what we do to earn a living. We all want to know management notices the effort we put into our jobs. And we all work better and harder when we feel appreciated.

CAREER OPPORTUNITIES MOTIVATE

Sooner or later someone in your organization will begin to scan the horizon for answers. Where will I be 5 or 10 years from now? What role will I play? What kind of future do I have with this company?

If an individual is ambitious and has a burning desire to advance within a company, keeping him or her with your organization may be unlikely unless you can show that person a career path for the deserving candidate. Even if it is unlikely a particular salesperson will reach a management position in the foreseeable future, the path will serve you well to show the opportunity possible to all whom you hire. This way, if people don't achieve a position in the future it will be because they didn't want it or weren't qualified. It won't be because the opportunity didn't exist.

AN EXAMPLE

Beal Trahan, his wife Pat, my wife Debbie, and I have been friends since before we were married. In fact, Debbie and I were married two weeks before Beal and Pat. We purchased our first home two weeks before Beal and Pat. My career and Beal's were on almost identical paths. Beal often tells people in his seminars that he originally was to be a computer analyst. However, every time he was with me, he noticed how excited and happy I was in sales, so he decided that's what he wanted to do as well. His first sales job was with National Cash Register, and I was his trainer/ team leader.

Beal is a quick study. He learned fast and quickly began enjoying success in the sales field. Now, let's skip forward in time 25 or so years. Beal is employed by a very large electric utility, whose name will go unmentioned. Beal works in the marketing department, where he facilitates training, evaluates programs for the utility's sales force and marketing department as well as delivers training. At that time, I was the VP of training and development for a security alarm manufacturer.

My job required I travel throughout North America, as I do today, conducting sales and sales management seminars for my company. One of those trips took me to the city where Beal and Pat lived. Naturally, I called beforehand to inform him I'd be in town. Beal invited me to stay with him and Pat at their home so we could catch up on what each of us was doing.

Beal and Pat and their four beautiful children were as happy as a family could be. Beal loved his work and his company. They both loved the home they lived in. Devout Christians, they loved the church to which they belonged. Beal was a deacon and Pat was involved with the Bible study group. The entire family loved the town they lived in, the schools their children attended—they were loving life. They were so happy it was almost disgusting. I was truly happy for them all.

About two months later I received a voice mail message from Beal, and by the sound of his voice, he wasn't happy. When I called him back, Beal told me about a letter his company sent to all employees.

Dear employees,
In preparation for deregulation, which no doubt will happen in the next few years, and as we no doubt will have to trim our workforce to compete in the competitive arena, we are rating all employees on a 1 to 9 scale.
    If your rating is a 1, 2, or 3 and if there is a position available for promotion, you will be considered for the

position. If your rating is 7, 8, or 9 and we are forced to lay off people, you will be the first in line for layoff.

Making matters worse, after receiving the notice, employees had to wait until their supervisor or manager ranked each employee. Supervisors and managers were forced to comply with rules, under which those rated 1 and 9 had to constitute 10 percent of the employees, those rated 2 and 3 must be 20 percent of the employees, and those rated 7 and 8 must make up the final 20 percent. In other words, if a department supervisor or manager had nine employees, no matter how good they were, one was told he or she was unproductive and was to be let go, and only those rated 1, 2, or 3 could be promoted.

When Beal finished reading the letter and explaining the program, I said, "By the sound of your voice, I assume you didn't receive a 1, 2, or 3 rating." "That's right," Beal replied.

"And I hope you didn't get a 7, 8, or 9," I continued.

"No, I didn't," Beal answered.

"Beal, were you expecting a promotion within the near future?" I asked.

"No," he shot back, "but I don't like being told I'll probably never get one!"

Beal's company, without trying, successfully demotivated the majority of its workforce with that letter. All those rated 8, 9, and 10 began looking for work. Ambitious employees rated 4 through 7 polished up their resumes as well. Even some of those rated 1, 2, and 3 began looking.

To the company's dismay, employee morale plunged. Those rated 1, who expected to get promoted, weren't. Many rated 1, 2, and 3 left for other companies. And, of course, the ones rated 7, 8, or 9 began looking for other employment.

Not everyone will or should make it into management. As I said earlier, being a great salesperson should be enough. However, almost no one enjoys the feeling of hitting a glass ceiling with no opportunity at all for advancement.

Here is a snapshot of an advancement ladder (shown from the top down) you can tell new hirees about. It vividly demonstrates the possibilities for a growing future with your company.

CAREER LADDER OF SUCCESS

Step 8. *Vice President of Sales.* This individual oversees all sales and reports to the company president.

Step 7. *Regional Sales Manager.* This manager oversees three or four offices and reports to the VP of sales

Step 6. *Sales Manager.* This manager oversees one office and reports to regional sales manager.

Step 5. *Team Leader.* The person is a perfect example of the program your company teaches, an excellent mentor and trainer who supervises a team of four or five salespeople and reports to a sales manager.

Step 4. *Senior Sales Consultant.* This is a top salesperson, who may be eligible for next team leader position if desired and qualified. Until then, the consultant reports to a team leader and a sales manager.

Step 3. *Sales Consultant, Level 2.* This consultant also reports to a team leader and a sales manager.

Step 2. *Sales Consultant, Level 1.* This person is just out of training, next step, level 2.

Step 1. *Sales Consultant, in Training.* This person is newly hired and remains a trainee until he or she learns the program and makes five sales.

(More about the ladder of success and compensation is found in Chapter 14.)

11

The Steps to Selling Success

My first book, *The Formula for Selling*, and its sequel, *The Formula for Selling Alarm Systems*,[1] focuses on what it takes to be truly successful in security alarm sales.

Success starts with you, specifically the image you have of yourself and the image you portray to the prospect. Maxwell Maltz, in *Psycho Cybernetics*[2] said, "One cannot act in conflict with one's own self image." Simply put, you are who and what you think and believe you are. If you see yourself as successful, self-assured, hard to say no to, and convincing, you are. If you see yourself as a failure, unconvincing, and unable to motivate a person to make a decision he or she was not already predisposed to make, you are that person you see in your self-image.

---

[1] Boston, MA: Butterworth-Heinemann, 1994 and 1996.
[2] New York, NY: Simon & Schuster, 1960. Copyright 1960 by Prentice-Hall, Inc.

Prospects tend to see you as you see yourself. If you project confidence, your prospects will have confidence in you. If you have doubts, the prospects will have doubts about your ability as well. So, correct image starts with how you see yourself, followed by how others see you.

If this sounds like a whole bunch of psychological mumbo jumbo, you must realize that the study of the power of our minds and how we see ourselves, self-image, has advanced far beyond Dr. Maltz's early theories. Sports clinics of all kinds use psychological programming, often called *visualization*, to improve the performance of all types of athletes. Self-image, how we see ourselves, and it's effect on our physical and mental ability to perform, is well documented and accepted.

You've no doubt heard the saying "you have only one chance to make a first impression." Ask yourself what kind of first impression you make when meeting with a prospective buyer? How are you dressed? Do you wear a dress shirt, slacks, and a tie if you are a man or an appropriate business dress or suit if you are a woman? Before you leave your home or office for an appointment, look in the mirror and ask yourself a couple of questions. If a salesperson looking like I do now knocked on my door, would I let the person in? Would I believe and trust this individual? Would I be perceived as a professional? Would I buy from the salesperson looking back at me in the mirror?

It doesn't matter if you think you're dressed appropriately, it's what your prospects feel that matters. You are better off and better prepared if you act on the side of caution and dress nicely, just in case how you are dressed is important to your prospects. If they don't care, being nicely dressed can't hurt you. If how you're dressed does matter, you're ahead of the game.

According to a study conducted by Michael Solomon, social psychologist and chairman of the Marketing Department at NYU's Graduate School of Business, people make 11 decisions about you in the first seven seconds after meeting you:

1. Your educational level.
2. Your economic level.
3. Your perceived credibility, believability, competence, and honesty.
4. Your trustworthiness.
5. Your level of sophistication.
6. Your sex role identification.
7. Your level of success.
8. Your political background.
9. Your religious background.
10. Your ethnic background.
11. Your social, professional, and sexual desirability.

All those decisions are made almost in a flash. I know people shouldn't be so quick to judge, but they do. This gives me more reasons why I must give a lot of thought to the first impression I make. The difference could be the difference in selling or not.

How punctual are you for the appointment? Does it matter if you're a little late? What if you got caught in traffic or delayed by an accident? Are these acceptable excuses for being late? Your prospect may not think so. You want to portray the image of a caring, concerned professional, a doctor of security.

The same is true with how punctual you are on a scheduled appointment. Some prospects get very upset if you are 10 minutes late for an appointment while others could care less.

Perhaps, the prospect had plans after your appointment, and now things are in jeopardy because of your tardiness. The longer you are late, the more irritable the prospect becomes and the more points you will have to overcome to make the sale.

Make it a point to always arrive for appointments on time or a little early, never late. That way you can't lose. If you are too early, use that time to drive around the neighborhood so you know more about the security risks that may affect the prospect. Drive around the corner behind the prospect's home. What's there? Are the homes similar? Is the area behind the prospect's home zoned commercial? Is there a school in the next block or an empty lot? The more you know about the environment of the prospective home, the better your recommendations can be. However, don't forget to get back to the house on time.

You have only one chance to make a first impression, make the best of that chance.

PLANNED POSITIVE ACTION

Planned positive action means what it says: Everything you do from the moment you arrive on an appointment has been planned, orchestrated to drive the appointment to a positive end, which should be an approved sales order. Know what you're going to talk about and in what specific order.

When seeing a prospect, I know the words I'll use to describe the features, benefits, and advantages of my company, product, and services; and I've checked my words to avoid saying anything that might hurt my chances of making the sale. I've loaded my presentation with words and statements that increase my chances of selling. I've eliminated words that could work against me.

Salespeople should role play their presentations in front of other members of the team. The purpose of this exercise is to uncover words being used by the salesperson that can be taken wrong, have a double meaning, or actually cause someone to lose the sale. Obviously I wouldn't want to say anything intentionally that could jeopardize making the sale, would I? Role playing helps identify problem areas and reinforces the positive aspects of the presentation I'm using. That's planning.

When I was in the field, selling, I can recall bouts I had with delayed intelligence. Delayed intelligence is what occurs when you're driving home or back to the office after an unsuccessful presentation. Suddenly, you recall something you forgot to say— something that, in retrospect, may have made the difference.

I can recall using a planned presentation and saw the sale being made by one single point, the prospect's "hot button."

Using the very same presentation on my next appointment, I vividly recall the next prospect not being moved at all by the feature that so impressed the previous person; however, the sale was made by yet another part of the presentation. The point is this: Had I not put on a planned presentation every time, I couldn't be sure that I would hit the one point that became the prospect's hot button, the one point that changes the appointment from no sale to a sale. In short, I use a planned presentation versus winging it.

As a professional I have learned what excites prospects and I use these in my presentation. I also have learned to avoid words that can work against me in selling. I approach selling as a profession like any other profession, requiring knowledge, skill, and a plan of action. All of which produces success on purpose, rather than by accident.

PLANNED PRESENTATION EXAMPLE

I train salespeople on a six step sales presentation:

1. Warm up the prospect.
2. Sell yourself.
3. Sell your company.
4. Uncover the need, sell the need.
5. Sell the problem the product solves.
6. Sell the solution.

Let's look at how these steps are delivered in a planned presentation.

Step 1. Warm up the Prospect

Warming up a prospect can be the most important step in the sales process. Your goal is to break the ice, establish a rapport, become more than the stranger who showed up on his or her doorstep. The warm-up also builds trust. Psychologically, people trust people they like. People buy when they like you, believe you, and trust you. The warm-up is designed to do all that.

How does one do an effective warm-up? Assuming you didn't start off with negative sales points by arriving late and the way you are dressed and groomed didn't offend the prospect, you've succeeded with the first impression. The next thing you should do is build rapport.

People like to talk about themselves and the things they enjoy doing. If you're observant, you'll quickly notice the things they like. Before ringing the doorbell, notice the landscaping. Is it attractive? Does it look like someone spends hours every week tending to it? If your answer is yes, then file that fact away until after you enter the home, because that may well be what you'll use to build rapport.

Once in the prospect's home, be observant. Ask yourself, "What do your prospects like to talk about?" Your answer often is on their walls. Are there pictures of their children or, better yet, grandchildren? If so, walk up and look at them. Ask, Are these pictures of your children? How many do you have? Depending on the couple's age, ask if the children still live in the home. Which school do they attend?

If you see evidence they like to ski, boat, golf, bowl, ride horses, or anything else like that, ask them about it. Ask how long they've been doing it, where they do it, when they do it, how they learned to do it, whether they compete while doing it, and so forth. Ask open-ended questions then listen carefully to what they say. Listen for situations that could make them more vulnerable to crime as a result of what they do.

For example, suppose the family loves to snow ski. Further suppose that, to do so, they must drive a long distance or fly to the ski resort. This means they must be away from their home as a family for a week or more. This means they probably had to make reservations to do so months in advance. They probably tell lots of people of their plan to go skiing again this year. They go to local ski shops to buy additional equipment.

All these things make it possible for them to become a target of a clever criminal who plans to break into their home while they're gone. Therefore, in addition to building rapport, you're gathering pertinent information that could help you protect them better.

When you allow prospects to talk to you about the things they love, they naturally begin to like you more. You've become a great conversationalist—one who listens a whole lot more than talks. You already are closer to making the sale.

Step 2. Sell Yourself

By virtue of your great warm-up, you already may have sold yourself. If they are saying to themselves, "My, this is a nice person," you are scoring points. However, depending on your experience, you could do more to sell your professional self.

Suppose the salesperson in question has been in the alarm business for five years.

> The Sales Pro: Jack and Mary, before we proceed on our task of determining your personal needs, I have found that folks like yourselves often want to know what my qualifications are, what qualifies me to make security recommendations to you. Because, after all, when a family chooses my company to protect themselves, I sort of become your employee. So, let me spend a moment telling you just a bit about my qualifications.
> I have had the pleasure of working with hundreds of families like yours over the past five years. I have learned much about what people like and don't like, which gives me a better feel for what should be recommended. I have revisited my customers after their systems were installed, enabling me to learn how to design the system in such a way as to be sure it works well in their homes and that they are comfortable with it. In short, I've learned an awful lot over the past five years about how to best pro-

tect families like yours. And I'm sure you will benefit because of my experience. Does that make sense?

If the sales representative is new to the company, I definitely do not recommend he or she make a point of that. You and I know a salesperson doesn't have to have years of experience to do a credible job for the prospect, but knowing the salesperson is brand new doesn't conjure up warm and fuzzy feelings.

So for the new representative, instead, either skip any conversation about your background or tie in your former work to what you're doing now. For example, suppose the sales representative sold insurance previously. Here's what he or she might say.

> The Sales Pro: Jack and Mary, before entering the security alarm field, I was in the insurance field. There were lots of positives associated with that field for me. First, I had the opportunity to meet with and help hundreds of very nice families prepare themselves in case of tragedy with insurance. If I did my job, and one of my clients suffered a loss in a burglary or fire, the insurance I provided for them went a long way toward helping them replace most of the things they lost. On the other hand, all too often I witnessed the sorrow one feels when losing possessions that cannot be replaced so easily, if at all, such as pictures of the children growing up, keepsakes, antiques, and the like. And, of course, if anyone was injured or died as a result, that was worse.
>
> I decided I wanted to be in a position that prevented the tragedy in the first place. A business where I could help people prevent a tragedy, so they wouldn't have to file a claim and wouldn't have to grieve the loss. That's why I decided to study to become a security professional.

(You see how that works? Give some thought to the words you'll use to tie in your former position to security, and then make the transition into the four-concern script to follow.)

The Sales Pro: Jack and Mary, during my study I found that people have to feel comfortable about four basic concerns before selecting a company to protect what is precious to them.

The four areas of concern are

1. The company.
2. The design.
3. The problem and its solution.
4. The investment.

The first area of concern is the company you will choose to do business with. Most people want to be sure the company they select is an expert in its field. We want to be sure the company knows what it is doing and is very good at it. Not many of us like being the guinea pig customer on whom the brand new, just started in business company is going to experiment. Isn't that so?

Next, and very important, we want to be sure the company we choose will stay in business, to serve us and to add on to, modify, and even service the product we purchased should we ever need service—5, 10, even 20 years in the future. Nobody likes the feeling of calling a company, two, three, or four years after purchasing the product only to find out it's no longer in business. Isn't that a terrible feeling?

Of course, because when it comes to the security of your home and family, you want and need the company to be in business as long as you need the service, not a day less. Doesn't that make good sense? So therefore, one of the areas of discussion today will be about my company.

The next area of concern, and oftentimes a confusing area, is the design of the system. You see, you want to be sure the system you select for the protection of your home and family accomplishes the intended goal without sacrificing your comfort. You don't want to feel like a prisoner in your own home. You want to be able to continue to enjoy your lifestyle, allow pets to live in your home as always, and have protection, yet use your home fully. Would you agree with that assessment?

Great, then we'll spend a few minutes today designing a system of protection that makes sense to your family—not a one-size-fits-all approach, which rarely fits anyone correctly, but a custom design that takes into account how you live in your home, providing ease and flexibility for your children and the same happy environment for your pets.

The next area of concern is the relationship between the problem we have to be protected against and the solution to the problem. I believe we all want to be sure the system we choose provides protection against the criminals and other life threatening problems. While doing that, we want it to be easy to use. Is that fair to say?

So we'll spend a few minutes discussing the problems against which we must defend you and your family and then explain the system that provides the solution to the problems.

The last area of concern, although certainly not the least area, is the investment. We all want to be sure we invest properly in anything we do. Isn't that so? Well, great. Let's look at the first area, my company.

The company I represent is ABC Security systems. We protect over ___ people, and we've been in business for over ___ years. We will install over ___ new security systems this year alone.

First of all, considering we protect over ___ people and have been protecting families like yours for over ___ years, wouldn't you think we know what we're doing? We are experts in the field of electronic security protection. Wouldn't you agree? And, considering ___ homeowners like you will ask us to protect what's precious to them, we must be a good company to do business with. We must do a great job. Wouldn't you think that's so?

Based on what I've told you about my company, is it safe to assume you would feel comfortable with ABC as your security company? By the way, here is a copy of my training certificate, indicating I successfully passed the training provided by ABC.

The second area we said we'd cover is the design. To do this correctly, we must assess your personal needs. We must look at your home the way a burglar does by doing a physical walk-through. First, is the personal assessment. (You will keep notes of the prospects' answers.)

Do you own or rent?

Jack: We're buying this home.

The Sales Pro: How did you hear about us?

Jack: We were contacted by phone by someone from your company.

The Sales Pro: Have you ever been a burglary victim?

Jack: No.

The Sales Pro: Do you know of anyone who has been a victim of a burglary or fire?

Mary: Yes, the family down the block was burglarized.

The Sales Pro: How did the burglar gain access to the home?

Mary: We never heard. We just know they were burglarized

The Sales Pro: The reason I ask is because burglars usually break into homes by entering through doors. In fact, over 85 percent of burglars break in through the door or open a door immediately on entering to prepare their escape, should they be detected by someone or should someone come home while they are still in there. They want to be sure they can escape.

When burglars break in through a window, they usually do so by forcing the window open or by breaking the window just enough so they can get to the latch and open it. They rarely break in by smashing the window and then climbing in over the broken glass. When they do, the burglar victim usually reports finding blood everywhere. Once breaking in that way, the burglar learns and doesn't do it again. Does that make sense?

Jack: Of course.

The Sales Pro: Was anyone physically hurt in the burglary down the block?

Jack: Hurt? No, I don't think so.

The Sales Pro: Well that's good. While no family wants a burglar even getting into their home, much less taking the possessions they've worked so hard to get, not having someone in my home hurt—my wife, my children, my pets—would be the most important thing to me. Wouldn't you agree?

Jack: Oh, yes.

The Sales Pro: Mary, what concerns you most about the crime problem?

Mary: When Jack goes out of town I feel vulnerable. I'm most afraid at night during those times, although I'm not very comfortable coming home after dark from a meeting either.

The Sales Pro: Jack, what concerns you most about the crime problem?

Jack: Before hearing what Mary just said, I would have said, someone getting into our home at night without us hearing them, and then waking up to a burglar with a gun. However, now I'm more concerned for my wife and family when I'm out of town. Mary, I had no idea you were so uncomfortable when I traveled on business.

The Sales Pro: When are you most concerned about burglary: during the day, at night, or when you're away?

Jack: At night, I believe.

The Sales Pro: When are you most concerned about the fire problem: during the day, at night, or when you're away?

Jack: I believe at night, once again.

The Sales Pro: Have you ever owned a burglar or fire alarm system?

Jack: No, we haven't.

The Sales Pro (if yes): What did you like most about it? (This doesn't apply here.)

The Sales Pro: Do you have house pets?

Mary: We have a dog.

The Sales Pro: What type dog do you have?

Mary: A poodle.

The Sales Pro: A male or female?

Mary: Female.

The Sales Pro: What is her name?

Mary: Mitsy.

The Sales Pro: Does Mitsy have free roam of your home?

Mary: Yes, unless we have company over, then we confine her to our bedroom.

The Sales Pro: How is Mitsy with your children?

Mary: She's just great with the children. She loves them.

The Sales Pro: That's the great thing about dogs. They give you unconditional love. Isn't that so?

Mary: That's true. Mitsy just loves to play with our children, and half the time she sleeps with them as well.

The Sales Pro: Does Mitsy stay in your home when you all are away for the day, let's say at work and school—when no one else is home?

Mary: Sure.

The Sales Pro: When no one is home except Mitsy, where does she stay or sleep?

Mary: Sometimes she'll sleep on our bed or on the chair in the family room.

The Sales Pro: Will Mitsy approach a stranger who enters your home or will she hide?

Jack: She'd probably bark a lot. She's very protective.

The Sales Pro: So Mitsy's a good watchdog, too.

Jack: Yes she is.

The Sales Pro: Jack and Mary, the reason I'm asking these questions is because it is important to the design of a good security system. I noticed when I first arrived, you have smoke detectors installed here, is that so?

Jack: Yes, we do. We actually have three—one downstairs and two upstairs.

The Sales Pro: Very good. Did you install them yourselves or did they come with the home?

Jack: Our builder puts them in all the homes he builds now.

The Sales Pro: That's great! Because you know why having smoke detectors is so important. If, God forbid, a fire broke out in your home, the design of the smoke detector is to detect the smoke and then sound an alarm early enough for you to gather together family members, and of course, Mitsy, and leave your home as fast as possible, before anyone is hurt or worse. Isn't that so?

The only thing wrong with your present situation is that, in the event everyone is away from your home on a given day or evening and a fire were to start, Mitsy probably would bark at the flames and smoke, attempting to defend your home. However, most likely, Mitsy would die in the fire. With our system, designed properly, we'd have an opportunity to save Mitsy and, of course, that is what we want. Don't we?

Mary: Yes, of course.

The Sales Pro: Does anyone in your household have special medical problems that may require emergency paramedic response?

Mary: No.

The Sales Pro: Neighbor response?

Mary: No

The Sales Pro: Do you ever sleep with windows or doors open?

Jack: Yes, on nice nights in the spring and summer.

The Sales Pro: Would anyone other than people who regularly live in your home have reason to enter your home without a family member with them?

Jack: No.

The Sales Pro: Are you concerned about any particular windows, doors, or area?

Jack: The back windows on the first floor worry me a bit, especially at night, and my master bedroom window closest to the patio cover.

The Sales Pro: Do you have a budget in mind for a security system?

Jack: No. We haven't really discussed it.

The Sales Pro: Who is your homeowner's insurance carrier?

Jack: State Farm Insurance.

The Sales Pro: By the way, the reason I ask this question is because, in most cases, insurance companies like State Farm give a fairly sizable discount to homeowners such as yourself when you take the precaution of protecting your home against the twin perils of fire and crime.

You have to wonder why an insurance company would do that? Why give you a discount when they already have your agreement to pay them (X) dollars per year? Why give you part of your money back? The reason is quite simple. Insurance companies know that a security alarm system installed by a reputable, high-quality company reduces the opportunity for a burglary and the chance of a serious fire, thereby reducing the chance they have to pay a claim. Naturally, they want to reward a behavior that potentially increases their profit. That makes sense, doesn't it?

Now that I have a better idea of your needs, let's take a walk around your home, looking at it the way a burglar might.

As you take the prospects on the security walk-through, start in an area where they can say no to additional coverage and you can agree. This technique allows you to take their buying temperature; in other words, how much they can or want to invest in a protection system. This technique is called the *spoon feed survey.*

THE SPOON FEED SURVEY

The spoon feed survey prevents you from suggesting more protection than the prospect is willing or able to invest in. It gives you a strong indication if the husband and wife are in agreement with each other. Are they willing to invest an equal amount? As just mentioned, start where it is easiest to say no, with your agreement.

> The Sales Pro (standing in the living room, at the front of house, looking out the window): Jack and Mary, as I look out this window, I see a couple of good things. The street appears to be well lit and this window appears to be highly visible from the street from all angles. Also, this seems to be the type neighborhood with a fair amount of activity out front, such as children playing, neighbors outside, and people walking pets. Is that about right?
>
> Jack: Yes, that is right.
>
> The Sales Pro: Also, you have kept the bushes in front of this window low enough to not provide a hiding place for the burglar who attempts to enter through this window. So, therefore, with all that in mind and thinking like a burglar, I believe a burglar normally would want a lot more cover than this window provides. While anything is possible, I believe a burglar is more likely to pick a door or another window to break in through rather than this one. Jack, how do you feel about this window?
>
> Jack: I think you're right. I can't imagine a burglar breaking into this window.
>
> The Sales Pro: Mary, how do you feel about this window?
>
> Mary: I agree also.

The Sales Pro: Great! We can skip this window for now. Remember, it always can be added to the system at a later date, should your feelings about this window change. (Repeat the process for all similar windows facing the front.)

The Sales Pro (standing by a window facing the driveway side): As I look out this window, I see a window that is slightly more vulnerable than the front windows. Obviously, the view of this window is not as good. One would have to be across the street and close to this side to see a burglar working on the window. However, because this side is wider and your driveway and your neighbors are on this side, it still can be seen. Thinking like a burglar, this window is easier than the front; however, I could still use more cover. But, if in a hurry, this window may do. Jack, how do you feel about this window?

Jack: I'm not convinced a burglar would pick this window either. It's still close to the front. (Personal note: What is this prospect telling you? He's saying, "Take it easy on me. I'll buy, if you don't make it too expensive for me." This is the purpose of a spoon feed survey.)

The Sales Pro: Mary, How do you feel about this window?

Mary: I'll go with my husband on this one. I believe the burglar could get in more easily through this window; however, I think it's more likely he'd go to the back or somewhere else first.

The Sales Pro: Great! As with the front windows, we know we can add them at anytime we wish.

As the location of the windows increase in vulnerability, tell them they do. Always end each statement with the question to the husband first, "How do you feel about this?" Then ask the wife. You're asking the husband first because if anyone doesn't want to invest much in the security system, historically, it's the husband. Also, the wife knows how to play this game. She knows if she can convince her husband to buy the system, she can get the upgrades and add-ons later—and she will—but only if she plays the game now.

After completing the walk-through survey, you return to the kitchen table.

> The Sales Pro: Now that we've walked through your home and made decisions about how it would be best to protect you and your family, do you feel comfortable with the design we arrived at?

This way, if one or both of the prospects has a change of mind about protecting or not protecting an area of the home, you can uncover it now, rather than face the "I want to think this over" objection later because they're not convinced the design is correct.

Listen carefully to how they answer your question. If the answer is a solid yes, then proceed to the next step. If there is a hint of hedging in their voice, stop. Tell them you detect they're not completely happy with the design. Ask what's bothering them, and then fix the problem by adding or deleting the area in question.

SELLING THE PROBLEM AND ITS SOLUTION

> The Sales Pro: Jack and Mary, now that we have a good idea of what your needs are, as I promised earlier, let's discuss the problems we must protect ourselves against. According to the Justice Department and the FBI, one out of three homes will be burglarized over the next 20 years. That means that, if there are 15 homes on this block, 5 will be burglarized. We just don't know which ones or when. A burglary is committed every 15.1 seconds.
> And the most frightening statistic to me is that over 50 percent of all murders occur during a burglary or robbery—over 50 percent. I think this is true partially be-

cause of the three strikes you're out law. As you know, that means a person who is convicted of three felonies gets life imprisonment. The punishment for murder most often is life in prison. So the burglar may feel he has less to lose if he kills rather than face the possibility of being identified and put away for life. Does that make sense? There are five basic type of criminals.

The professional, the one we read about in books, is glamorized in movies. This is the cat burglar. You must know that this burglar doesn't just burglarize any home. The professional is looking for a victim who has hundreds of thousands of dollars worth of jewelry—millions of dollars worth of fine art. He doesn't want your wedding rings, your fur coat, your TV or stereo. In fact, Jack and Mary, I can assure you this burglar isn't breaking into my home. I have nothing to steal that this guy wants. If he did break in, seeing what I have, he'd probably feel sorry for me. Maybe even leave something behind. (Give them a big smile.) However, I don't want to be presumptuous, do you feel this burglar would burglarize your home?

If the answer is yes, ask what the professional burglar would be looking for. That's when they'll tell you about the coin collection they didn't mention earlier or the wall safe that houses $500,000 in jewelry. If their answer is "No way!" then smile and continue.

The Sales Pro: Great, then we don't have to worry about this guy, do we? We do, however, have to concern ourselves with the next one, the vandal.

Vandalism is getting worse than ever before. The reason is partially due to the increase in gang activity. Sometimes the initiation to get in a gang is to commit a crime. The new gang member is driven to a neighborhood, a home is picked at random, and he is instructed to "trash" the house. What he may do is crush delicate furniture, kick in TVs, rip open stuffed furniture, pull out the stuffing, pour ink on the carpet and fabrics, slash draperies, paint ugly graffiti sayings and slogans on the walls, plug up drains and let the water run, and sometimes start fires.

Homeowners who have been through a vandalism attack have reported flashbacks. They say they come home at the same time of day, with the sun or shadows appearing the same and just know when they open their door they'll see their home destroyed as they did when they were vandalized. Obviously we must protect you and your family against this type criminal. Wouldn't you agree?

The next type criminal is a criminal I don't like talking about. It's a very sensitive area. I'm referring to the predator. Suffice it to say, this person preys on women, children, and older folks. It's obvious we must protect you against his type.

The fourth criminal and the one responsible for the majority of burglaries is the drug addict. The criminal drug habit today runs between $300 and $1000 dollars per day—every day. When you consider the addict needs drugs every day and then multiply the lower amount, $300, by 365 days per year, that is over $100,000 per year just to support this habit. Forget about food, rent, utilities, and other bills we all must pay every month, this burglar needs $100,000 just to support the habit.

When you further consider that a junkie is lucky to get 10 cents on the dollar for stolen goods, such as $30 for a VCR worth over $300 or $25 for a camera worth over $300, he has to steal stuff worth more than 10 times this reduced value. So, to maintain a $300 per day habit, the addict must steal over $1 million worth of goods each year. The average retail dollar value of a residential burglary is approximately $1200. Which nets $120 to the burglar. To support his $300 per day habit he must burglarize three homes every single day of his life—more, if his habit is bigger. You can see why there are so many burglaries, can't you? This guy is dangerous, often high on drugs or desperately in need of drugs and obviously is someone we must keep out of your home. Isn't that so?

The last criminal type is sad. I look at six-year-old children as someone I must protect against the bad guy, not someone I should be protected against! Last year in southern California, a six-year-old and two eight-year-olds broke into a residence and, in the process of stealing, almost killed a baby in a crib. Do you remember reading about that in the paper?

Ask a policeman this question: If you were responding to a burglary in process and knew for sure someone would be in the home with a gun, which would you rather find—a 12-year-old with a gun or a 40-year-old with a gun? Which do you think the cop would pick? The 40-year-old, right? Of course. The 12-year-old has no fear. He's invincible and probably will not receive anywhere close to the same punishment if caught. He'll kill in a minute. So, unfortunately today, we have to protect ourselves against children.

Are there any questions Jack and Mary?

Now that we know who we must protect you against, let's talk about solutions. Let's talk about how easy our system of protection is to use and, then of course, to own.

Here is where you explain or demonstrate your product. Remember, KISS (Keep it Simple, Salesperson).

THE CLOSING QUESTION

The Sales Pro: Jack and Mary, the system we just discussed, completely installed according to the schedule of protection we decided on earlier, which includes (repeat what is to be installed), is only $___ plus $___ per month. When would it be best to install it, are mornings or afternoons better? (Now, shut up! The next one who speaks buys.)

Here is a quick formula to keep in mind:

$$CI + PPA = SOP$$

The correct image (CI) + planned positive action (PPA) = success on purpose (SOP).

12

See the People— Lead Generation

Even the best can't sell if they have no one to sell to.

Teaching your salespeople how to continually find prospects to sell to is paramount.

Have you ever heard the saying, "Good things come to those who wait"? In sales you should add, "However, only those things left behind by those who hustle."

"Give a man a fish and he'll have food for a day. Teach a man to fish and he'll have food for a lifetime." No truer words have been spoken when it comes to selling. You can start with a staff of better than average salespeople, give them leads every day for a year or two, and before you know it you've created lead junkies, salespeople who no longer know how to fend for themselves, how to feed themselves.

Don't get me wrong, I'm not against giving my salespeople help in the way of a lead. However, the leads I provide should

147

not be enough for them to feed their families on. The leads I provide should be the bonus I give them for finding prospects on their own. If I have the capability of producing enough leads to comfortably support 5 salespeople, then I probably should hire 10 salespeople.

In developing a sales organization, it is my job or the job of the manager I hire, to teach the salespeople whom I've hired to prospect for leads. Every chance I get, I'll take my salespeople to a seminar and give them or get them to buy books that cover the topic of lead generation. They can't sell unless they have someone to sell to.

FINDING PEOPLE TO SELL TO

The following paragraphs will cover numerous methods of finding people to sell to. However, let me give you a few words of caution first. No one method listed here will work by itself often enough to make a big difference. Second, there is no way your salespeople can utilize all of these methods simultaneously. Have them pick three, four, or five of their favorite methods and then work them consistently and hard. Just as important, you must manage the process.

THE 15 + 15 + 15 RULE

Let's start by talking about the 15 + 15 + 15 rule. The rule begins by suggesting your salespeople send 15 pieces of mail to 15 targeted prospects every day.

In my home and I'm sure yours, direct mail has a name, *junk mail*. Now I wouldn't want to suggest your salespeople send 15 pieces of junk mail to anyone, because the prospect will likely do what I do and what over 75 percent of the people who receive junk mail do—throw it away, trash it without even opening the envelope, file it in the round file.

The national average response rate of junk mail is approximately half of 1 percent. Pretty dismal. If one mails direct mail by the thousands and hundreds of thousands, it works. However, your salespeople can't and won't do that. So how can we make the mail your salespeople send more effective? First, let's ask ourselves how we know the mail is junk mail before opening it? How can we feel so confident throwing it away without first finding out what's inside?

Here's how. The envelope has "you have won" on the front. Ed McMahon's picture, "special offer inside," and other such phrases. The envelope has a postage meter stamp or is bulk rate mail. The envelope has a return address or name I don't recognize. All of this allows me to make a fast decision that it is junk and that I can throw it away.

You see, I don't have a friend who sends me letters using a permit mail machine or bulk rate. My friends usually use a real lick-em, stick-em stamp. My friends usually don't have my name on mailing labels. And my friends don't preprint messages all over the envelope. They usually use the paper inside to tell me what they want to say.

There are three basic rules for direct mail to be effective:

1. The prospect must *open* the mail.
2. The prospect must *read* the mail.
3. The prospect must *take action*.

If the prospect doesn't open my mail, all else is worthless. I could have placed a cashiers check for $1 million inside and unless someone opens the letter, no one benefits. Therefore, the very first thing I must concentrate on is getting someone to open the letter I send. Here's how you can be sure the prospect will do that. And I'll guarantee, if you do exactly as I say, 90 percent or more prospects, when receiving your letter, will open it.

1. Send your mail in a wedding invitation size envelope with no logo or advertising of any kind on the outside.
2. Place a lick-em, stick-em stamp on it. Don't use a postage meter or bulk mail.

3. Handwrite the prospect's name and address on the envelope. (By the way, if you want to make this easier, you can purchase computer software today that will print your envelope and letter in your handwriting.)
4. Do not put a return address on the envelope. (Why do we put return addresses on envelopes? To get them back if the addressee doesn't receive it, right? Do you want your own junk mail back? No? Then don't use a return address.)
5. Send the same letter or slightly different letter in the same type envelope to the same address three times over a 45 day period; in other words, every 15 days. Repetition has been proven to work. By the third time, the prospect will think he or she knows you or your company. The person will recognize your name. You have to know that big companies invest millions of dollars every year to get customers to know them, to recognize their name, to build brand awareness.
6. Target the prospect you should mail to. Ask yourself, where do the prospects live that are more likely to be responsive to my offer? Who is likely to buy my product? You can find their names by using a criss-cross directory. By targeting your mail in this manner, you're not wasting your time on areas of town where you can't sell.

So now for the test. Let's see how we did against the first rule: Open it. Ask yourself honestly, if you received a letter in the mail as just described, would you open it? Attendees at my seminars all say they would open the letter. If that's true and you utilize the method just described, you will have fulfilled the first requirement of direct mail.

The second rule is to get the prospects to read the mail. First of all, don't write a long-winded letter. No one will read it. Handwrite the letter on notepaper, the type you would fold over once to fit in the envelope. Don't include a business card, reply card, or anything else that could automatically tell the prospect, "Oops! This is junk mail."

Handwrite a short note or use the computer software that prints the note in your handwriting. The note should explain what you plan to do, and what you expect of the prospect. Direct mail experts say that prospects most likely will read the first couple of lines of the first paragraph or the PS. If either grabs their attention, they'll read on.

I know a salesperson who enjoyed more than an average degree of success with a similar mail program. His letter went like this:

> Dear Jack and Mary,
> I'm writing a letter like this is because I believe it has a better chance of being read by you. My business is one of protecting families just like yours against the twin perils of fire and crime.
>
> I'll be calling in the next few days to establish a convenient time to share some vital information with you. Please talk to me when I call.
>
> Sincerely,
John Smart

The first sentence of the letter said to the prospect, I tricked you into reading this. Then the letter went on to say why. Finally, the letter said what the salesperson expected of the prospect: "Talk to me when I *call*."

You see, this salesperson didn't expect the prospect to follow the third rule of direct mail: Take action. He believed it was unlikely the prospect would. Therefore, he took the responsibility for taking action: he called.

The reason you can't rely on the prospect taking action is simple. Your prospects live in the same nation as you and I. It happens to be the largest nation in the world: Procrastination. We all procrastinate. We all hear advertisements on TV or the radio or read them in the newspaper and do nothing about them, even when we are interested. We plan to do it some other time—later on, when we get around to it—and nothing happens.

Adopt this rule: Never send a letter to a prospect unless you plan to call him or her. By calling, you give the prospect the opportunity to act instead of procrastinate. You make it easier for the person to take action. You are doing the person a favor. Scratch out rule 3. Prospects won't take action. Don't count on it. That takes care of the first 15 of the 15 + 15 + 15 rule. Send 15 pieces of mail to targeted prospects every day.

The second 15 of the 15 + 15 + 15 rule is to *call* 15 people every day, the 15 people you mailed to three days ago is a great start. You told them you would call, so now do it.

The mail you sent serves as a warm-up to a normally cold call. You're now making a warm call. You should call the prospect each time you send a piece of mail, not after the third piece, every time.

Next, expect an objection when you call. Don't be so naïve as to believe the prospect always will be happy to hear from you. Occasionally, that's true, but more often than not, you'll hear this most typical of objections, the objection we all must have been taught in our mothers' wombs, "I'm not interested."

I'm not surprised when I hear this. I'm prepared for that objection. Learn to say this in response.

Me: When you say you're not interested, are you saying you're not interested in buying anything, is that what you're saying?

The Prospect: Exactly, I'm not interested in buying anything.

Me: Great! Because I'm not interested in selling you anything. I can make you two promises. First, the information I will share with you and your family when we get together will prove valuable to you and your family. And second, I won't demonstrate anything or attempt to sell you anything unless you ask me to. And, of course, if you're not interested in buying, you won't ask. That's fair isn't it? So when can we get together? Would tonight at 6 or tomorrow at 7:30 be better?

If you do this, you'll get appointments, not all of the time but enough to make it well worth the time you invested. You also have to be able to fulfill the two promises made. Later in this book, I'll tell you how. This is the second 15 of the 15 + 15 + 15 rule.

Rule 3 is shake 15 hands every day. Go see the people, belly to belly. Canvassing is by far the fastest and easiest way to make sales today. Knocking on doors puts your destiny squarely in your hands, not in the hands of the mail carrier, the phone company, and not in the hands of a procrastinating prospect. You're in charge.

In fact, knocking on doors gives the procrastinating prospect the opportunity to get out of the land of procrastination and take action. As you knock on doors, you'll find the people who have been meaning to get around to calling you. People who have wanted to buy but haven't. You'll make sales right at the door. All you have to do is develop a script (what to say) and then "get off your seat and on the street." Your customer is waiting.

DOOR KNOCKING STATISTICS

I have worked with sales organizations and their salespeople throughout North America and have found the following to be somewhat of a worst case.

1. If you knock on 50 doors in a targeted neighborhood, you'll be able to speak to 15 people on average. Some of the 35 people will not be home or won't come to the door or only the children or a household worker is home. Fifteen people will speak with you.
2. When speaking to 15 people using a good script, you'll be able to set three or four appointments.

3. Depending on your closing average, you'll close two to three sales.

The whole process is rather mechanical. Numbers work for you. If you want to improve the numbers, canvass at a time when more people are home. Saturdays and Sundays are best, because people usually are home on weekends. Weekends are gold mine days for residential salespeople.

Become a fixture in the areas you canvass. Get to know what's going on: who is moving in, who is in the process of selling a home, who is doing improvement work, who just had a pool installed. The better you know the area, the more effective you'll become. Invest in your long-term future. It'll pay dividends.

SELLING BY THE NUMBERS

Sales is a numbers game. You get paid for everything you do. For example, let's suppose, using the preceding example, you knocked on 50 doors, spoke with 15 people, made four appointments, and then made three sales. Let's further assume you earn $200 per sale made. This would mean that you earned a total of $600 (3 × $200).

If you divide the $600 you earned by the 50 doors you knocked on, you get $12. Which means you've earned $12 for every door you knocked on. So ask yourself this question: Suppose I was in your town, offered to follow you into a targeted neighborhood, and said I will give you $12 for every door you knock on, whether the residents are home or not, talk to you or not, buy from you or not. How many doors would you knock on today? As many as you can? Until your knuckles are bloody? You bet you would.

The reality is, because you must knock on the 50 doors to speak with the 15 prospects to get the four appointments to make three sales, you do earn $12 for every door knocked on. The numbers are the numbers. Improve the ratio and you earn more per door. It's just that simple.

Selling by the numbers is a healthy mind-set to acquire. Let's say you are a 50 percent closer. This means you will sell, on average, to half of the people to which you make a presentation. If you earn $200 for each sale made, you earn $100 for every presentation you make. Unless you can show me how you can skip the people who don't buy and only see those who will buy, the fact remains you earn $100 per presentation. By the way, if you ever figure out how to eliminate the no-sales, only seeing the buyers, give me a call. We'll go on tour together and both get rich.

REFERRALS

The bonus great salespeople receive in sales are the sales they make as a result of the first sale. Sales pros always ask for and get referrals. They know it's their life's blood. Sales pros get referrals more easily because they know they can and their assumptive style in asking produces for them.

When should you ask for a referral? Ask for referrals at the time of sale, at the time of a no-sale, when the installation starts, a few days after installation when visiting the customer to explain system features, and then anytime you speak with the customer by phone or in person. In other words, ask often.

How should you ask for referrals? If you get used to using the two promise answer to the I'm not interested objections when calling prospects for appointments and if in fact you share information as part of your presentation to your prospects that one day could avert a tragedy in their home, then you will have the right to ask for referrals in the following manner.

The Security Professional: Jack and Mary, would you agree that the information I shared with you today could, one day, avert a tragedy in your home?

Jack and Mary: Yes.

The Security Professional: And would you also agree that, even if you were not going ahead with the system for your protection, you benefited from the information I shared with you?

Jack and Mary: Yes, that's true.

The Security Professional: Great! Who is the first person you know I can share this valuable information with? (Your head is down, pen in hand ready to write on your lead form.)

You now have a better reason for your customer to refer you to others. Everyone benefits from the life saving information you'll share. Everyone they know and care about should be given the same benefit they'll derive from your visit. Isn't that so?

During my years in the field, selling belly to belly, easily 70 percent of the sales I made came from referrals of one type or another. I enjoy visiting people who want to see me, who were referred by someone they know and trust. That type of sale is the easiest.

The road to superstardom and big money in sales is the referral road. However, you have to make sales first. The more sales you make, the more referral sources you'll automatically have, if you work them.

BIRD DOGS

A bird dog, to a salesperson, is someone who brings him or her leads, someone to sell to, like the hunting bird dog points to or flushes out birds to shoot so food can be put on the table.

Real Estate Agents

Real estate agents are obvious bird dogs. They know people who *are buying* a home. I emphasized *are buying* because it's an important point. I don't need a real estate agent to tell me who has bought and closed on a home. I can purchase a list that gives me that information. I want to know before everyone else does.

Make life real simple for the agent. All you need is the name and present phone number of the person who is purchasing a home but has not yet closed on it. The agent doesn't even have to convince the home buyers they should see me. Just tell me who are buying which homes and how I can reach them today. I'll take it from there. If I make a sale as a result of the lead, I'll reward that agent financially. If the agent is able to schedule an appointment for me with a home buyer who mentioned the desire to purchase an alarm system and I make the sale, I'll reward the agent even better.

If you choose this lead generating method and work diligently on it, you'll find yourself with several good bird dogs in the real estate business. Many will come from the same agency.

So then how do I get the financial reward to the agent? Mailing the check is easy but not the correct answer. Deliver the checks to them personally: one check, one referral per envelope. If you've received several leads from a particular agent that resulted in sales, don't batch them together. One check per referred sale is best. It looks like more. It feels like more.

Ask if you can make the presentation of referral rewards at the agent's office during their weekly meeting. Some office managers will permit this, some will not. Ask permission to make the presentation, who knows, they may say yes. If they agree, mix up the envelopes. If you have two checks for Laura, three for Bill, and one for Sally, call Laura to the front of the room and present her with one check. Thank her for helping you protect her client against fire and crime. Call Bill next, give him one check, and thank him as you did with Laura.

Repeat the process until you've given all the checks you brought with you and caused Laura and Bill to come up and get money several times. Think about what the other agents in the room are thinking about now. "What gives?" an agent asks the agent next to her. "How come they're getting checks?" "How can I get in on this? Show me the money."

Property and Casualty Insurance Agents

WIIFM is the world's favorite radio station: What's in it for me? This is the station the insurance agent listens to as well. The agent is not interested in helping you make a living but in making his or her own living. Therefore, if I'm to develop a relationship with an agent, I must show how he or she will benefit.

Consider this scenario, Joe Q. Smith is an insurance agent who represents insurance lines such as Aetna, Chubb, and Lincoln. Twenty years ago, Sandy bought a car and got her insurance through Joe Smith. A year later Sandy bought her first home. She called Joe Smith's office and spoke with Joe's assistant, Millie. She told Millie she bought a home, and after a few simple questions, Millie quoted the rate over the phone. Sandy took it.

Five years later, Sandy was doing well. She bought a bigger home. She's already on her third car through Joe's agency. Sandy called, spoke to Millie again, received a quote for the insurance, and went ahead with it.

Over the past 20 years, Sandy has bought three homes, a vacation home, a boat, and owned at least two cars insured at all times, all covered by Joe, who hasn't had to do anything for the business he has received. Sandy's daughter is now driving at high insurance rates. Sandy referred her brother and mother to Joe's agency as well. Life is good for Joe Q. Smith.

Last month, Sandy arrived home from dinner with the family and discovered they had been burglarized. The next morning, Sandy called the insurance agency to report the burglary. As usual, she spoke with Millie. Millie arranged for an adjuster to go to Sandy's home, and after some time, Sandy received a check from the insurance company for the full loss. With the exception of the feelings all people get when they are burglarized, Sandy is happy with the results.

Yesterday, Sandy received a letter from Joe's insurance agency. The letter notified Sandy her insurance policies were going up in cost by some 30 percent because of the burglary loss. How do you think that makes Sandy feel? Do you think she understands the position of the insurance company? Or do you think she now hates Joe Q.? I believe the latter is highly possible.

Sandy may now decide, for the first time in 20 years, to shop around for another insurance company. And, no doubt, Sandy will find a more competitive rate. Now, all of a sudden, Joe is losing Sandy's insurance business—easy business. Joe also will lose the insurance on Sandy's cars, vacation home, her daughter's car, Sandy's brother's business and all that business has grown to, and Sandy's mother's business, too. Today is not a good day for Joe Q. Smith.

You could have helped Joe prevent the loss of a good client. You can help Joe keep his other clients. When Joe helps his clients protect their homes and families with the installation of a security system, provided by your company, he is minimizing his customers' chance for a loss as well as his chances of losing a valued client. That is one benefit for Joe Q. Smith, insurance agent.

Second, you can help Joe's agency earn a bonus, which in some cases is greater than the money earned on policies all year. When his clients protect themselves with a security system, they are less likely to suffer a loss that Joe's agency has to pay. Aetna, as well as most other underwriters, pay agencies a large bonus if they are able to reduce the losses their actuary departments have predicted for the agency. Help me save money and I'll make it worth your effort is what the underwriter is saying. You can help Joe earn his bonus by installing alarm systems in the homes and businesses he insures. That makes sense doesn't it?

Last, every time you sell because of a referral given by the insurance agent, hand carry a thank you check to him or her. The agent will appreciate the sentiment.

Inspection Services

Most cities have one or more companies that do inspections of existing homes for new home buyers. They spend hours in the home looking for problems. When the inspection is completed, a report detailing everything found is mailed to the prospective home buyer.

Guess who knows a purchaser who will be going to close on a home even before the home buyer knows? You guessed it. The inspector knows. He or she knows if the report on the home being inspected is satisfactory and the purchase will happen. The inspector also knows who the new purchaser is and how to contact that person today, long before any list gets the buyer's name.

In 1996, when I purchased my home in Littleton, Colorado, I employed the services of an inspection company. My purchase was contingent on a satisfactory inspection. After the inspection, I received an excellent report and began to finalize on a closing date. A week or two after the inspection, I received a telephone call at my office in Jacksonville, Florida, where I lived at the time. The call was from an insurance agent in Colorado. He introduced himself and said he heard I was purchasing a home in Littleton, Colorado. When I said I was, he asked if I wanted a quote for homeowners insurance. I said, "Yes."

I bought the policy without ever calling another agency. I was busy. The quote sounded reasonable. I didn't know anyone else in Denver to call for insurance, so I bought it from him. It was just that easy. I wonder how he knew I was buying a home in Littleton, Colorado? Want to make a guess?

Other Referral Sources

Exterminators The ones we pay to keep bugs out of our homes, make good bird dogs. They are inside of people's homes all the time. They may know about a burglary, a fire, remodeling, or anything else that may make their customer a prospect for us.

Locksmiths If the locksmiths aren't in the alarm business too, they make good bird dogs.

Glass Companies Sometimes, in the process of a burglary, windows are broken. Guess who knows about the burglary shortly after the police?

Police Police officers obviously know when a burglary has occurred and so know who is a prospect for a good security alarm system. You'll learn, however, police officers are not suppose to refer alarm companies. I say they're not *supposed* to refer alarm companies because I know they do. They do when they feel real good about the company they're referring.

Small town police departments are the easiest to work with. They generally have a closer relationship with the people in their towns. They know them on a more personal basis. They also have the time to be involved in crime prevention. Get to know them. Explain your company and its goals to the officer. Ask for their help wherever possible.

Crime Prevention Departments Crime prevention departments of bigger cities are the place to focus your attention. Their job is to educate the public on how to prevent becoming a victim to crime. They regularly put on crime prevention meetings for neighborhood groups, church groups, and other organizations. Ask them how you can help. Develop a relationship.

Fire Fighters Fire fighters are great believers in what a good fire alarm system can do. Educate them on the difference between the ionization sensors sold in stores and installed by builders in homes and high-quality photoelectric smoke sensors. There is a big difference between the two, a difference that could make the difference between living or dying in a home fire. Of course, first you must educate yourself about the difference.

Clubs Rotary, Elks, Kiwanis, neighborhood watch groups, Parent-Teacher Associations—all of these organizations have something in common: They meet monthly, often for lunch, sometimes for breakfast or after dinner. All their members live somewhere, most with families. And most of the people who conduct and attend the meeting are prospects for you. Finally, all of these groups include a person, a volunteer, who was foolish enough to accept what appeared to be an easy task, which is to find 12 interesting speakers willing to speak to their group at a regularly scheduled meeting for approximately 15 minutes on a subject they'll all be interested in. Doesn't that sound easy? Not hardly! Finding 12 speakers this year willing to speak for free for 15 minutes is a difficult if not near impossible task.

You and your salespeople can help. The following is a complete script on how to locate organizations to speak to and what to say at the meeting. If done correctly, you'll receive the respect of the organizations you speak to, and your credibility will skyrocket. The organization will feed you a breakfast or lunch, depending on when the meeting is held and, very important, you'll make sales as a direct result of the meeting.

FIRE SAFETY SEMINAR

Fire safety is an interesting and life saving topic. It can be covered well enough in 15 or 20 minutes and will be appreciated by the members. After doing a couple of fire safety seminars, you will find yourself being sought out by other organizations to speak to their groups, and in case I forgot to mention this, you'll make sales.

To get started, contact your local chamber of commerce for a list of all organizations listed with them. The list should have the names and phone numbers of the president, vice president, other officers, and probably the program's chairperson. Send each a letter introducing yourself and your willingness to conduct a meeting on the subject of fire safety. Follow up the letter with a phone call to the program's chairperson, and you're on your way. The following is the meeting I would conduct.

> Good [morning, afternoon, evening], my name is ___ and I represent ___ Security Alarm Company. Our business is protecting families, homes, and businesses from fire and crime. I am here today to talk to you about fire—about what you can do to prevent fire, what you should do, and as important, what you should not do in the event you are in a home when a fire starts.
>
> I know and you know some basic truths about fire, things we've learned since we were children. Also, we need to discuss some things about fire that have changed. To start, however, I'm going to ask a couple of true and false questions of you and I would ask you to answer by simply raising your hand.
>
> Now before I ask the first question, is there a volunteer or regular firefighter in the room? (If there is, request the person not to answer as you know he or she knows the answer; however, the reason you're asking is because such people might not know the answers and you are saving them some embarrassment. Once they realize what you've done for them, they'll love you for life.)
>
> The first question is an easy one, one I'm sure you all know the answer to. Here goes.
>
> Question 1: If you are trapped in a house on fire, the air nearest the floor is always safest. All those who say that is true please raise your hands. (Raise your hand to encourage them to do so.)

All who believe the statement is false, raise your hands. (Once again, raise your hand to encourage those who believe it is false to do so. Most, if not all, will answer true.)

Well, as you can see, most of you answered true. The correct answer is false. (Now you have their attention.)

The answer is false because today our homes are stock full of items that are chemically produced such as nylons, Dacrons, plastics, and other chemically produced products that, when burned, give off a heavier-than-air deadly gas that sinks to the floor. Therefore, the air nearest the floor actually is more deadly.

In a fire you have two things to be concerned about. First, you have the heavier-than-air gas going to the floor, approximately 18 inches and less, and the superheated poison air descending from the ceiling with temperatures exceeding 500 degrees. The safety zone is right in between. The problem is that most of us have been taught to believe we should get down on our bellies and crawl out when, in fact, that very action could end our lives.

Question 2: Fire travels from object to object, room to room. All those who say that is true please raise your hands. (Raise your hand to encourage them to do so.)

All who believe the statement is false, raise your hands. (Once again, raise your hand to encourage those who believe it is false to do so.)

Answer: The correct answer is false. Heat and smoke rise. Once hitting the ceiling, which is made of a fire retardant material, sheetrock, smoke and heat flow across the ceiling until they cover the entire ceiling area and then begin descending. As they do so, heat and smoke will spill out into other rooms doing the same thing. Once the heat comes in contact with a highly flammable object, such as drapery, a new fire starts. This could be several rooms away from the original fire. Newspapers lying on the floor next to the object that originally caught fire may never burn, while objects on the other side of the house are consumed by the flames. (Note: At about this place in the discussion, have someone from your company pass a form around the room for participants to register for a "free survey.")

Question 3: If I were asleep in my home and a fire started, the heat from the fire would awaken me. All those who say that is true please raise your hands. (Raise your hand to encourage them to do so.)

All who believe the statement is false, raise your hands. (Once again, raise your hand to encourage those who believe it is false to do so.)

Answer: Unfortunately, this is false, too. Descending heat and smoke produce the opposite effect: One is rendered unconscious from the smoke and heat. If you breathe in the superhot air, your lungs will burn and death will result. This is why fire chiefs throughout the country have begged and pleaded with the American public to invest in smoke detectors and are now pleading with those with smoke detectors to check and change the batteries in them regularly.

Question 4: In case of a fire, all members of the family should get out the best way they can and then go to any safe spot outside the burning home: True or false?

Answer: This answer is false. An important safety training rule to adopt in every home is to establish a family rendezvous point. That is a place where we all agree to meet in the event of a fire. This rendezvous point can simply be the neighbor's front lawn across the street.

This rule is important because it has happened that all family members managed to get out of a home on fire; however, since one of them, perhaps a small child, is unaccounted for, the father, mother, or both go back into the home searching for the missing member and die in the fire. If we all meet at the same place, we can count heads and prevent this needless loss of life.

Question 5: If I am in my bedroom on the second floor and a fire starts, should I immediately open my door and exit the house as fast as possible? True or false?

Answer: False. If there is a fire in your home, opening a door from your bedroom to the hall or rest of the house can produce an explosion that can result in serious injury or death. If you saw the movie *Back Draft*, that is what happens. The colder air from your room mixes with the hotter air on the other side of the door, and a back draft explosion results.

The proper way is to feel the door on your side first. Feel it high up. If it feels hot to the touch, do not open it. If it doesn't feel especially hot, brace your foot against the bottom of the door and then open the door a few inches, enough to feel the air on the other side. If you feel hot air, close the door and exit through your window. If not, you can proceed out of the door staying low yet above 18 inches from the floor.

Question 6: If I can't exit by the door, should I plan to open my bedroom window and jump to safety?

Answer: This is false again. Jumping out of window may result in death or severe injury. If your second floor window sill is 12 feet above the ground, and you are 5 foot 2 inches tall, at full arm extension hanging from the window sill, your feet are only a little over 4 feet from the ground. Dropping 4 feet to the ground is much better than jumping 12 feet to the ground.

Question 7: If I am asleep and the fire alarm sounds or someone somehow gets my attention awaking me, should I get up fast and leave the house quickly?

Answer: False. Getting up quickly is the problem. Because heat in excess of 500 degrees could be descending from your ceiling, sitting up in bed as you normally would to get out could very well put your head right into the descending heat. One breath could prove deadly. The correct way to respond to this emergency is to roll out of bed, gaining no height. Staying low, crawl to the door checking it as mentioned already.

Question 8: If a fire starts,

a.   Should I attempt to put the fire out first?

b.   If I can't put it out, should I call the fire department immediately and then get out as fast as I can?

c.   Since smoke and heat rise, should I lay down on the floor with my head as close to the floor as I can and crawl out of the house.

d.   None of the above

Answer: The correct answer is d. You should not attempt to put out the fire. In a fire, every second is critical. According to the National Fire Protection Association, you have less than two minutes to escape alive from a home on fire.

Calling the fire department before you get out of the house wastes valuable time and subjects you to possible injury or death. Get out first, then call the fire department. Smoke and heat do rise, however, and as mentioned, the heavier-than-air gases given off when chemically produced products burn sink to the floor. Crawling with your head at least 18 inches above the floor is the correct and safe way out of the house. Small children should not crawl if, when in a crawling position, their heads are lower than 18 inches.

Now that we know a bit about what to do and what not to do, let's spend a moment or two talking about everyday things around our homes.

Question 9: By a show of hands, how many here own a clothes dryer? Of course, everyone except those living in apartments have one. When is the last time you cleaned the dryer? And, before you answer, when I say cleaned, I mean pulling the dryer away from the wall, removing the screws holding the back panel on; the panel that says warning, hazardous, electrical shock may occur. When is the last time you took that panel off and vacuumed the inside of the dryer? No one?

Answer: Well, if you did, you would have found the wires and motor covered with a lint blanket, very much like the one found in the lint filter when you clean it. You see, the motor in the dryer requires air to operate like all motors in appliances. It therefore pulls in the air around the dryer, pulling dust with it. The dust collects around the wires and motor so all it takes is a minor malfunction and you have a fire. Your dryer should be cleaned on a regular basis to prevent this potential fire problem.

Question 10: By a show of hands, how many of you own an automatic coffee maker, like a Mr. Coffee? How many of those coffee makers are unplugged right now while you are here at this meeting? How many of you unplug the coffee maker at all?

Answer: You may remember, when you took the coffee maker out of the box it came from the store in, there was a tag connected to the power cord that said to unplug the coffee maker after each use. The reason it says that is because the coffee maker makes coffee through the use of a controlled short. Simply, the coffee maker shorts the positive side of 110 volts with the negative side, which causes heat and eventually fire if left that way too long. All it takes to start a fire is for the coffee maker's device that removes the short to malfunction and you have a fire. The coffee maker companies realized this, which is why they placed the warning on the cord.

Fire safety is a subject that must be taken seriously. Fire knows no friends and exhibits no prejudices. Fire can be and all too often is deadly. The more you know about how fire starts and spreads, and what to do and, more important, what not to do in a fire, the better. We at ___ Security take our responsibility of protecting people from the twin perils of fire and crime seriously, which is why I'm here today.

If you would like to receive a free fire and intrusion survey of your home to learn specifically what you can do to minimize your risk, simply indicate your wishes on the form going around the room. I'll be happy to call you and set an appointment for a private consultation.

Thank you. (End of meeting.)

Learn this program. Contact the organizations and get started. You will make sales, I promise.

OTHER METHODS OF FINDING PROSPECTS
Flyers and Door Hangers

There are right ways and wrong ways to market using flyers and door hangers. The wrong way is to walk up to a house to hang the door hanger hoping no one is home. The right way is walk up to a house and knock on the door. If someone answers, hand that person the flyer or door hanger, explaining what it says and why you're there, which of course, is to make an appointment to tell them about the opportunity you have for them.

You'll be surprised how many times prospects will be able to speak with you right then and there. You'll be further surprised how many sales you'll make.

The best time to distribute door hangers is immediately on making a sale. Go to the houses on either side and across the street from the home you just sold. In an average block, you'll find 12 or more homes. Knock on each door with the door hanger in hand. If the prospect comes to the door, you say this.

The Sales Pro: Hi, my name is ___ with ABC Security. The reason I'm stopping by is because we are installing a security alarm system for the ___s [next door, down the block, whatever]. And because I assume you are a security conscious neighbor, I wanted to alert you that you will see our truck in their driveway or out front. I didn't want you to be concerned, it will be just my company installing a protection system for them. Also if you hear a siren sounding, it'll be just us testing the alarm. OK?

You may be wondering why the __s decided to invest in a security protection system and how affordable a system like the one they're getting is. It would only take a few minutes for me to explain it to you, would you like to do that now or would tomorrow at __ be better?

You'll be surprised once again how many people will say, "Sure, how about now" or "I've been meaning to get an alarm system, come in."

Everyone You Know

Don't let happen to you what has happened to too many security sales professionals I've met. Tell everyone what you do. Don't miss anyone.

Here is an example of what could happen. Suppose you have been in the alarm business for approximately one year. Suppose you're invited to a party, a high school reunion, or the like. When there, someone you know but haven't seen for some years walks up to you and says hello. Next he says, "What are you doing these days?" To which you reply, "I'm in the security alarm protection field, with ABC." To which he replies, "You sell alarm systems?" You say, "Yes I do." He says, "I'm so sorry. I wish I knew. I just purchased an alarm system a couple of months ago. In fact, my mother, sister, and brother all bought from the same company within days of each other. If I had known that's what you do, we all would have purchased from you." How would you feel, terrible? Of course. People would rather do business with people they know if given the choice.

Tell everyone you know. Get your yearbooks out and start jotting down names. Make a list of everyone you know and contact them. Tell them what you do for a living and ask for their help. Anyone they know or may contact who expresses the need for or information on a security alarm system is someone you want to make contact with. Your friends will love to help, if you ask.

13

Develop Leaders—
Lead, Follow, or Get
out of the Way

Now that we know more about how to locate, interview, hire, train, and motivate a sales force, we must revisit an earlier topic: planning. More than one well-intentioned business entrepreneur has fallen victim to unplanned growth. And usually the business pays dearly for it, sometimes resulting in the failure of a once successful company. To head off some problems that, at best, can temporarily derail your company and, at worst, kill it, you must revisit a five year or longer forecast of growth plan.

Go into your office, close your door, take out a piece of paper, and imagine five years from now. How big could your company be. How many units will you be producing? How many salespeople will it take to sell that volume, considering a factor for new salespeople who have not yet jump-started and salespeople you hired previously who are failing and will be gone soon. How many salespeople will you have? How many offices will your company grow to? One particular dealer I work closely with has 12 offices in five different states and will double that number according to his growth plan. So how many will you have five years from now?

Considering the WAG (wild assed guess) you're now building, what will your organization chart have to look like to manage the size your organization has grown to? As you grow, your need for upper and middle management people to manage and control the organization becomes apparent. You will need sales managers, training managers, installation managers, service managers, general managers, finance managers, administrative managers, possibly national sales managers, and perhaps a "tiger team," which consists of one or more trained pros you send into new cities to jump-start offices, hire and train the first employees, and then move on to another city to do it again.

All this costs money, and the money must come from somewhere. However, for this chapter, let's focus on sales and sales management.

If you're fairly new in the business and have the ability to manage people, including salespeople, you no doubt will do it yourself. However, as you grow, you may find your time being stretched. You won't be able to do the job adequately.

The first management post you may find yourself filling, depending on your own strengths, is an operations position, someone who manages the installation service effort while you manage sales and general management, finance included.

As sales and volume grow, depending on your choice of a high-end, low-volume or low-end, high-volume market, you'll be faced with the same soul searching decision I faced when I owned a security alarm company. The question is this: Because of the business, finance, and accounting decisions that must be made when running a bigger business, do I hire a sales manager to run the sales effort of my company or do I hire a general manager to handle the business side while I handle the sales management?

Your answer to this question can be found more easily by asking yourself another good question: What do I do best? Are you a much better business manager than a sales manager or a better sales manager than business manager? Are you very detailed oriented, bottom-line oriented?

Let me tell you a true story, my story, which may help make the point. In 1974, I was vice president of the security alarm division of a rather large local security guard company in the New Orleans area. When I first accepted the position, the security alarm division was doing rather poorly. Sales for the previous year was around $175,000. The alarm division employed one and a half salespeople and one installation crew member. The half salesperson was the second salesperson they could never manage to hire and keep working. One salesperson, Frank Clement, was knowledgeable and a good closer. Most of the sales produced were produced by Frank. My instructions by the company owners were quite simple: Make it grow.

Once I learned what an alarm system was all about and how to best sell them, we began to grow. The training program demonstrated earlier in this book in part comes from that growth. We learned the hard way, through trial and error.

By the end of the first year, sales almost tripled. Management was happy with the progress. Suddenly I found myself wearing many hats. While trying to grow the sales force, I was general manager, installation manager, service manager, finance manager, and so on.

In 1977, I negotiated to buy the alarm division from the security guard company. Within one year of the purchase, sales reached over $1 million. The average system we sold at the time went for approximately $1250, which means we were selling and installing around 800 systems per year—a lot of alarm systems at that time. Don't forget, we were charging $1200 for them, not giving them away. Also, owning an alarm system was the furthest thing from most people's minds.

Soon we employed anywhere between 8 and 10 (two person) installation crews, which required we purchase, equip, and maintain 8–10 installation vans. (Subcontract installers didn't exist yet.) Our service department grew from none to three full-time service technicians, a service dispatcher, and a service manager. Our building requirements changed three times, requiring we move, renovate a space, and add furniture.

Along the way, I discovered a need for a patrol response team, someone to answer my customers' alarms faster than the police. My company owned its own central station. (Contract monitoring was just beginning.)

The patrol division grew quickly from 1 car 12 hours daily (6 PM to 6 AM) to 10 patrol cars daily, 4 of which were 24-hour-a-day cars. The company now employed a vice president of patrol, numerous lieutenants, and so forth. On the alarm side, it employed a sales manager and 8–10 salespeople at any given time.

I was going crazy. And I wasn't doing what I did best and what made me happiest. It was difficult finding and keeping good sales managers.

Finally, one day, I received a phone call from Mitch Resnick, the president of a franchise organization of which my company was part. He asked me how I was doing, and I told him I was frustrated, tired, near burned out, and driving my wife, my family, and my employees crazy.

After a moment of thought, Mitch said to me, "Lou, I think I may have your solution." To which I said, "Great! What is it?"

"Fire yourself," Mitch said. "What?" I replied. "That's the craziest suggestion I have ever heard. Mitch, I don't have time for this." I said.

Mitch continued by asking me who was the best sales manager I knew. Who was the best motivator of salespeople I knew. "And he's right in your building," he said. Of course he meant me. "Sure," I said. "I know I can do the job, but I have so much else to do. This job requires a whole lot more."

"That's right," he said. "Fire yourself, take the sales manager's job, and hire someone to take your job. Someone who is good with detail, who loves paperwork, who probably couldn't manage a sales department if his life depended on it, but does what he does very well." Mitch was right. And that's what I did.

In your growth plan, you must take this possibility into account. Don't let your business manage you. You must do what you do best and hire people to do the other things necessary for success. However, all this comes at a price.

Which brings me right back to the five year plan. Your plan should anticipate growth and the need for management levels. By doing that, you won't commit too much of the profit on each sale to the sales manager or anyone else, only to have to take it back when additional mangers are needed. Your people won't understand or be happy with a cut in pay. By planning ahead you prevent the problem.

14

Keep Management Focused on Taking the Next Hill

Empower your management team to perform. Set realistic goals for salespeople and then manage them to their goals. Remain the excited, motivated person you had to be in the beginning then require the same from your management team. Don't become stingy. Share the wealth. Well-rewarded and -motivated managers produce results, assuming you hired the right people. Which brings me to another point. If you promote someone from within the organization to a management position, do so with a parachute clause built in—a back door, if you will.

Sometimes, despite your best effort and his or hers, someone doesn't work out, the person can't cut it as a manager. This is no disgrace and shouldn't be treated as such. Let the person know, going into the job, that it is possible he or she is not right for the job or the job is not right for that person. Agree to be open in your thinking, to discuss problems if they crop up. And agree on an exit strategy if the job doesn't work out for either of you, an exit strategy that doesn't require losing the once valuable employee altogether. The back door to provide is a graceful, no loss of ego, way back into sales or wherever the manager worked prior to the promotion.

Here is a recent example of what can go wrong if a back door isn't in place. In 1995, I met a recently appointed sales manager at an annual sales rally. The young man was bright, bubbling with enthusiasm, and anxious to prove his worthiness for the job bestowed on him.

Less than two years later, I received a phone call from him. He called to express his thanks for the help I provided, but told me he was quitting the following Monday. I asked why. He admitted the pressure of the job was getting to him. He wasn't achieving as he and as his superiors had hoped. When I asked him what he was going to do next, he said he was accepting a position as a salesperson with a local competitor. I tried but couldn't talk him into staying.

Some months later I heard from him again. He was still working with the new company, and he proudly told me he had been salesperson of the month three months in a row. He was doing very well.

Had the original company, who promoted him to sales manager because it felt he was good as a salesperson and could transfer his talents to others, developed a back door for him, he'd still be there. His sales performance would have benefited the original company instead of its competition.

Everyone isn't cut out to be in management—and that's not bad. Compare the sales field with acting for a moment. Actors spend an entire career honing and perfecting their acting skills. The rewards they receive are partially the personal satisfaction one gets in knowing one is good. The Academy Awards, and others like them, recognize the best of the best. Of course, producers recognize the best by asking the actor to make movie after movie for incredible money. An actor can be an actor his or her entire career without ever directing or producing, think of Jack

Nicholson. Is he a success if he never produces or directs a movie? Winner of three Academy Awards, you bet he is.

A professor in a university may never become the dean or head of a department and may not care. Being the best at what one does is the reward. And the pay usually is commensurate with the talent. It's important management understand this philosophy and promote it. Find ways to recognize and spotlight achievement.

For management to be focused on taking the next hill, it's mandatory we bring in new managers and make them part of the master plan, our five year plus goal. Together, develop and refine the intermediate goals that will get you to your five year goal. Build a reward system into the plan, whereby the managers benefit along with the company as the goals are achieved.

The easiest and probably best way to accomplish this is to structure the managers' compensation plan around the stated goals. For example, let's assume my company's five year plan is to build to 10 offices selling on average 200 units each per month. (If this sounds like a lot to you, I know at least three companies right now that are easily on track toward this goal.)

We'll assume this company is new or has radically changed the direction in which it was going, recognizing the paradigm shift and that the newly restructured, reengineered company is a high-volume company. The one office location the company has is selling approximately 70 systems per month at present. And today is the first day of the new five year plan.

If you did some simple math, 10 offices divided by five years suggests you open two offices per year; that is, if simple math works. More realistic planning suggests the first year of the next five may be devoted to getting the first office producing 200 orders and, at the same time, building the team to develop the other nine offices.

By month nine of the first year, you should have identified the first manager who will help you grow the other offices. This person's job now is to work with you on the plan for the second office. Where is it going to be, and why there?

Next management should assemble a small "tiger team." A tiger team consists of one or two salespeople/team leaders who can go with the manager to the new location to jump-start it. These are salespeople who, when placed in any city, can sell starting the first day. They become the role models and trainers for the people you'll hire for the new location. The goal is for the tiger team to develop people who can replace them in the new location, so they can move on, according to the plan, to the next office location. If one tiger team member exhibits management ability, he or she may be promoted to the sales manager's position for office 2.

The general sales manager's job is to oversee both offices, keeping them on schedule. He or she also must replace the tiger team members at the first office location. Once the team leaves to open office 2, sales at office 1 is affected. We can't let this happen, so part of the growth plan includes replacing the tiger team's sales.

Year 2's plan is in place; that is, to open and develop two offices, growing both to an average of 200 orders each. By the end of year 2, production is forecasted to be 600 units to cover sales from three offices.

Year 3 continues on the same course set for year 2. Add two new offices, each producing an average of 200 orders per month. By the end of year 3, you should now have five offices, selling in the neighborhood of 1000 systems per month.

Year 4's plan may get a bit more aggressive. With the key team players in place, it should be possible to speed up the growth process to three offices, selling 200 units each, by the end of year 4. Total sales for the company is now 1600 units per month.

Year 5 continues on track with year 4: Add three offices, selling 200 units each. If you've been adding up the offices in this model plan, you've come up with 11 offices not 10. This wasn't an accident. I always plan to exceed the goal if I'm to hit it. Who knows, perhaps one of the locations would turn out to be a dog. Perhaps, the combined averages would not quite reach 200 units each. This fudge factor in planning enables me produce results instead of excuses.

So, let's look at what this plan suggests I need in the way of management. First, I need a general sales manager. By the time my second office opens, I'll need a sales manager for that office. Before the end of the second year, I must have three managers. The first manager is managing office 1 as well as the managers for offices 2 and 3.

Year 3's goal called for two more offices and two more managers. This means, by the end of the year, my general manager's responsibility has grown to managing four sales managers located in four cities—plus running office 1. Unless this person is superhuman, he or she probably will need to hire a sales manager for office 1 and assume the position of regional or general sales manager or regional vice president. Along the way, other responsibilities had to be shifted to new management people, such as responsibility for installation crews.

As the owner of the company, don't forget the basic principles of the Peter principle; that is, everyone has a level of competency. We all can reach a point where we no longer are competent, we can't do the next higher job.

With this in mind, you may find yourself in a position where you must hire, from outside your company, the person who will assume the role of regional vice president. The manager you hired in the beginning may not have the ability to captain the ship you've just built. This isn't an absolute; however, you should prepare for it.

Compensation for your manager should be based on that person hiring, developing, and managing salespeople as well as achieving goals established by you, volume as well as growth. Be prepared to increase that person's compensation if he or she exceeds the goals set by you.

Figures 14-1 through 14-5 show how the sales organization charts might look, assuming the preceding plan. These organization charts should give you a feel for how the sales management structure grows.

Figure 14-1.   Year 1 Organization Chart

Within the sales team itself are other layers of sub-management necessary to provide salespeople closer supervision and mentoring. This position is often referred to as *team leader*.

The team leader position also serves as management training (see Figure 14-6). It provides a ladder for ambitious salespeople to climb as well as additional income potential. The team leader continues to sell everyday; however, he or she also works with team members, either having a new salesperson ride along

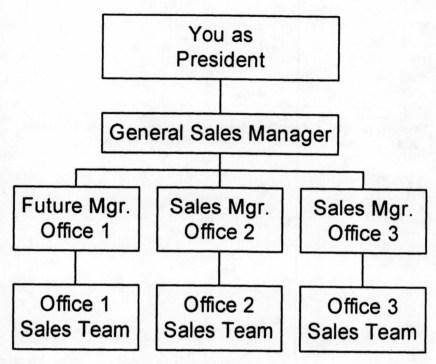

Figure 14-2. Year 2 Organization Chart

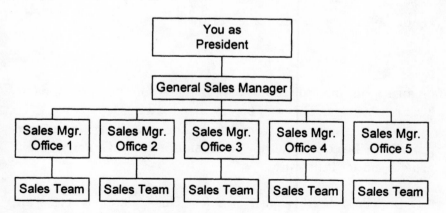

Figure 14-3. Year 3 Organization Chart

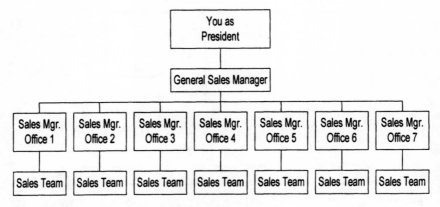

Figure 14-4. Year 4 Organization Chart

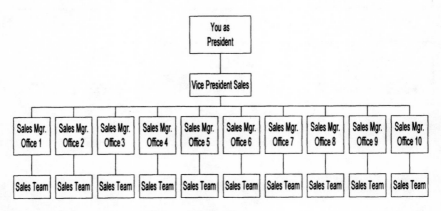

Figure 14-5. Year 5 Organization Chart

on an appointment or riding with the new salesperson on his or her appointment. This will be discussed later.

Many salespeople want to see the possibility for career growth in the company they're considering. See Chapter 10 for growth ladder illustration.

Step 8. *Vice President of Sales*. This person oversees all sales.

Figure 14-6.   Where the Team Leader Fits In

Step 7.   *Regional Sales Manager.* This manager oversees three or four offices and reports to the VP of sales.

Step 6.   *Sales Manager.* This manager oversees 1 office and reports to regional sales manager.

Step 5.   *Team Leader.* This person is the perfect example of the program your company teaches, an excellent mentor and trainer who supervises a team of four or five salespeople and reports to the sales manager.

Step 4.   *Senior Security Consultant.* This is a top salesperson, who may be eligible for the next team leader position, if desired and qualified. Until then, the senior consultant reports to a team leader and the sales manager.

Step 3.   *Security Consultant, Level 2.* This consultant reports to a team leader and the sales manager.

Step 2.   *Security Consultant, Level 1.* This person is just out of training, next step, level 2.

Step 1.   *Security Consultant, in Training.* This person is newly hired and remains a trainee until he or she learns the program and makes five sales.

15

Know the Enemy (the Competition)— Its Strengths and Weaknesses

As in war, to win, to stay alive, you must know your enemy. The better you know how your competitor operates, its strengths, its weaknesses, the better are your chances in direct competition. However, I don't believe in knocking my competitor. It doesn't work. In fact, it is more likely to work against me than help me.

However, knowing my company's strengths as compared to the competition's and knowing the competition's weaknesses allows me to build a presentation designed to emphasize my company's strengths while exposing the competition's weakness.

There is a big difference between understanding your competitors and constantly worrying about them. Before going into the security alarm business, I worked for National Cash Register

(NCR). While it's important to be aware of the enemy, if you spend all your energy looking for land mines and snipers in the trees, you'll make very little, if any, progress.

STAY FOCUSED

On a particularly hot August day in New Orleans, the humidity-laden air hung heavy over the city, permeating everything it came in contact with. Chuck Andres sat in his large corner office of the NCR building at the corner of Causeway Boulevard and Interstate 10. He was staring out of the window, as air conditioning compressors strained to remove moisture from the air while making a feeble attempt at cooling the building. Feeling my presence as I entered his office, Chuck glanced over his shoulder and said, "Hi Lou." Then in an almost inaudible voice said, "that's the fourth Sweda truck I've seen pass today."

It was 1969 and NCR enjoyed an almost 80 percent market share in the cash register business and was making inroads into the computer and accounting machine business. However, sales for that year and the year before were flat and turning downward. Although NCR owned market share, some upstart new companies were eroding that share. Swarming around it like irritating gnats, companies like Sweda and Anchor were biting off pieces of NCR's market as the corporate management was pressuring Chuck to increase sales. Chuck was at a loss about what to do.

Chuck was a veteran NCR general manager, having started in sales some 30 years earlier. Somehow, over the years, Chuck lost some of his edge. Changes in equipment happened at blinding speed. Mechanical equipment was on its way out and computers and electronic equipment on its way in. It was all becoming too much for Chuck. He missed the old days when things were simpler.

The New Orleans office held a lot of sales talent, but Chuck just didn't know how to develop it. He was tired and getting aggravated by the constant buzzing of the gnatlike competitors. He wished they would just go away and leave him alone. One day I walked in the office and Chuck was gone. The word was that he retired. No fanfare, no going away party, he just disappeared into retirement.

After Chuck, we in sales were introduced to an assortment of new general managers. All arrived full of vim and vigor, and all left on a stretcher, babbling to themselves. The New Orleans office was quickly developing a reputation as a career killer. The "Big Easy" lifestyle of New Orleans was often just too much for the new executive. A sharp-looking, confident executive on the way up the corporate ladder would walk in the building, and a broken shell of a person would crawl out. It was an awful sight to behold. And sales continued its downward spiral.

Then Bob Tiffe arrived as the new general manager. Bob was six foot two and walked with an easy air of confidence. He had a quick warming smile, and unlike his somewhat stuffy predecessors, Bob was friendly and engaging. He roamed the building constantly talking to everyone, offering assistance whenever needed. Bob was a refreshing breath of cool air in a previously humid, dank environment.

Soon after, Bob brought in Frank Leon as cash register sales manager. Like Bob, Frank was a ball of energy. He genuinely loved the salespeople and showed it. Frank spent time meeting with our eight member cash register sales group, assessing the local situation. He quickly determined that enthusiasm was waning, and a check up from the neck up was in order. Frank rode with his salespeople and his enthusiasm and confidence soon rubbed off on us.

Between the efforts of Bob and Frank, sales at NCR in New Orleans began to rise. Bob and Frank knew we had competition and knew their strengths and weaknesses. They prepared for the enemy but, more important, kept us focused on our sales goals. Due to the management of Bob and Frank, NCR New Orleans experienced a complete turnaround.

OBSTACLES ARE SEEN ONLY IF YOU TAKE YOUR EYES OFF THE GOAL

Chuck and the managers who followed him were consumed by the competition, that was all they could see. Chuck went so far as to count the competition's trucks as they passed the building. Bob and Frank acknowledged the competition's presence and recognized its potential, but then focused on attaining sales as their goals. And as the leaders go, so go the troops.

The situation at NCR is a great example of how important management is to the success of an organization. Bob and Frank created a fun atmosphere combined with high expectations and driven by personal then corporate goals. Under Bob's management, all of the managers reporting directly to him worked closely with their sales teams. They taught by example. Frank, my manager, rode with each of us at least twice a month. And when he did, he took advantage of the one-on-one time to personally coach and critique performance. However, I never felt put down. Even when I failed, Frank used my failure as a lesson to improve my future performance.

Frank and Bob weren't obsessed with the competition; however, they made sure we were all totally aware of the competition, its strengths and weaknesses. When you know your competitors' weaknesses, assuming you are strong where they are weak, emphasize that strength, explaining the importance of the feature to your prospects.

16

Compensation Plan

The subject of compensation can be approached in numerous ways. However you approach it, plan ahead for the management levels and support needed to produce sales. It is better to start paying what you know you'll be able to afford than to change the compensation plan later on. When you lower compensation, regardless of the reason, you risk losing good employees.

In the high-volume business, straight commission plans are the norm. High-end selling usually requires you pay a draw against commission or a salary plus commission. The standard in the direct sales industry—if one could say there's a standard— is to pay an approximately 15 percent commission on high-end residential sales. The same 15 percent applies to add-ons to a previous sale.

High-volume salespeople in the security industry usually receive commission on the unit or package sold. The typical package includes two door sensors, one passive infrared, one interior siren, the control and touch pad necessary to make the system work, and connection to the monitoring center. Today, most companies offer this package for from nothing to $99 installation plus $24.95 per month without maintenance or $29.95 per month with maintenance included.

If the company supplies no benefits, such as 401K, life and health insurance, vacation and sick pay, the commission paid for the package ranges from $75 to $125 for a company provided lead, and $100 to $150 for a self-generated sale (where salesperson found the prospect on his or her own). Also, a commission is paid when the salesperson sells more than the base package. That commission averages approximately 15 percent of the additional amount sold.

From this point local creativity rules. Most companies agree it is in their best interest if salespeople sell more rather than less in a given month. Even though the salesperson is on straight commission, overhead expenses are incurred for every person employed. Obviously then, the more the salesperson sells, the less per sale the fixed overhead expense is; therefore, the more profitable the salesperson is to the organization.

For this reason most companies increase commissions based on volume tiers. For example, the company will pay $100 per sale to the salesperson for from 1 to 14 sales in a month using company provided leads and $125 for sales using self-generated leads. If the salesperson sells between 15 and 19 orders in a month, the company will pay $125 for all sales made from leads provided by the company and $150 per sale from self-generated leads. If the salesperson sells 20 to 29 orders in a month, the company will pay $150 and $175, respectively, for each type of sale. Those who sell between 30 and 49 orders receive $175 and $200, respectively, for the two types of sales. These amounts go up to $200 and $250 when over 50 orders are sold in a calendar month. This type plan rewards volume. It takes care of the top dogs, keeping them with the firm.

Next in line in the commission plan is the team leader. The team leader may receive $10 and $20 per sale made for everyone on the team as well as sales commissions for his or her own sales.

The sales manager is paid an override per sale also; however, I recommend you also structure a bonus based on achieving goals. The override may be in the neighborhood of $20 to $25 per sale plus an achievement bonus of $5 per sale if the goal is reached. If the sales manager has other management duties as well, such as installation, administration, and so forth, you'll have to pay a salary for that portion of the duties.

When you reach a size requiring you employ regional sales managers, their compensation can be based on unit sales in their region with or without a salary. The same is true for the vice president of sales.

Just for fun, let's do some math. First, assume the average commission paid to salespeople including the superstars equals $170 per sale. The team leader receives $10, the sales manager receives $25, the regional manager receives $10, and the vice president receives $10. In total, that equals $225 per sale made, plus bonus potential for the vice president, regional manager, and sales manager. Work the numbers into your overall plan in the beginning and you'll know where you're going and what to count on.

AVERAGE COMPENSATION EARNED

No doubt you'll be asked what is the potential for income with your company. I can say from firsthand experience, a top salesperson can earn in excess of $100,000 per year. The average salesperson earns approximately $45,000–55,000.

A team leader will average close to or with the top producer if he or she is good.

A good sales manager will average approximately $75,000. A top one will earn as much as the top sales producers. (By the way, it is almost a given that sales managers earn less than top sales producers.) Regional managers and the vice president naturally will have to make more than the sales manager or they'll reconsider the job.

DEVELOP THE DESIRE TO WIN

I've had the privilege and pleasure for the last seven years to travel all across North America, meeting with security alarm dealers of all sizes. OK, I'll admit traveling isn't always a pleasure. But it is a pleasure and interesting to meet as many independent dealers as I have.

However, it never ceases to amaze me how you can feel the difference between a go-go, successful dealership and one that's so-so. You can feel the excitement in the air. Successful organizations have managed to power up the people who work for them. They're happy, motivated, and have a burning desire to kick the competition's butt. Plain and simple, they love to win. They expect to win. No doubt about it.

So how does one develop that feeling in an organization? It starts with you, the active working principals of the company. You have to fire yourself up. You have to become excited and stay that way. It doesn't matter how you personally feel. It doesn't matter if you have a headache. Your organization requires you to be up. You're the leader. If you don't, you'll have even better reasons for having a headache.

You must not tolerate negativity in your organization. It takes only a little negativity to ruin what you're trying to build. Look at it this way. Suppose I placed a full glass of clear, clean water in front of you. If you are thirsty, you'd have no trouble drinking it, would you? However, suppose I took a small pin, inserted it in a pile of horse manure and then stirred the water with the pin. Would you want to drink the water now? No? Suppose before stirring the water, I shook the pin well, attempting to throw off as much manure as possible prior to stirring, and then stirred the water with the pin. Would you want to drink it? Probably not, right?

The point is this: Just as it doesn't take much manure to ruin a glass of water, it doesn't take much negativity to ruin an organization. Don't allow it to exist. Stomp it out, eradicate it like the disease it is.

Negative people seem to thrive on causing others to join their negativity. New people are especially vulnerable to the negative employee. And, what's worse, the negative person often is immune to his or her own poison. Such people are much like a disease carrier. They live almost unaffected by the poison they spew while everyone around them dies. Why am I so sure this is true? Because, early in my sales career, I had a close encounter with this very problem.

At the time I was employed as an account manager for a major international corporation. Each salesperson with the company was assigned a quota and a territory to work. Other than at sales meetings, we rarely spent much time together.

Every year the company put on a convention. The convention, usually in a warm, beach location, was all inclusive. Airfare, hotel, meals, golf, and entertainment were free. The convention, for all practical purposes, was a two week, all-expense-paid vacation. On top of that, earning a trip to the convention each year you were qualified, weighed heavily in advancement decisions. To qualify, salespeople were required to sell in excess of 125 percent of their annual quota.

One particular year I qualified for convention along with one other member of our 12 person sales team. The other salesperson, Bill (not his real name), was someone I knew, but hadn't spent much time with other than at sales meetings.

The day before we were scheduled to depart for convention, Bill asked me if I would pick him up on the way to the airport since he lived on the way. I agreed. Shortly after picking up Bill, he began complaining. First, he complained about the traffic, "Why didn't the city do something about synchronizing traffic lights?" He complained about the other drivers around us, "Where did everybody get their drivers licenses anyway, from a catalog?" He yelled at other drivers and scowled the whole way to the airport.

As luck would have it, once we arrived at the airport, all of the close-in parking was taken. We had to park at one of the remote lots. Bill complained furiously about the inconvenience. Why didn't the airport board create more parking spaces closer in?

Bill and I were assigned seats in the back of the plane, just in front of the row of seats where smoking was allowed (this is when smoking was still permitted on all flights). "Sure!" Bill complained, "we get put in the back of the plane. Right in front of smoking. We sold our butts off all year long, you'd think the company would get us better seats. And how does the smoke know not to come forward to us, huh?" Bill complained to the flight attendant about our seats, to no avail.

As normal, after takeoff the flight attendants passed through the plane offering beverages. Bill started complaining again. "Great," he said, "we have to pay for mixed drinks. As much as we've done for the company you'd think they would put us in first class or, at worst, buy our drinks." Bill was not happy, and I was becoming increasingly unhappy also.

When we arrived at the convention, we discovered that, due to the size of our company, conventioneers were spread out into three different hotels. All the meetings and festivities were at one hotel. Of course, as luck would have it, we were housed in the hotel a block and a half away from the host hotel.

Bill didn't like that either. "How come we're housed two blocks away?" Bill complained. "We made our quota. How come those other salespeople got to stay at the host hotel? Who do they know? It might rain! Then how will we get to the meetings? This is not fair!"

By the end of that day I hated my company and I hated the free, all-expense-paid vacation I was on—all in just one day. Bill's constant negative attitude infected my normally positive attitude. A couple of more days with Bill could have caused me to quit my job.

Fortunately for me, after Bill went to his room to unpack, I found other convention attendees I'd met the year before, happy conventioneers. The negative programming I had been exposed to by Bill began to wear off. I loved my company again and was proud and happy to be at convention.

Successful salespeople exposed to an influence like Bill, through passive learning, can acquire the same negative attitude. Those who once considered the glass half full will begin to see the glass half empty. Unbeknownst to them, the negative person can adversely affect their behavior and their careers.

Are there negative people like Bill in your organization? Could they be infecting you and others within the company? People like Bill are psychological disease carriers. They can survive in an organization despite their negative attitudes with no apparent harm to themselves. However, everyone else around them dies!

I'm big on formulas. The formula for selling, if you read Chapter 11, is CI + PPA = SOP. The formula for a successful sales organization is Career Path + Money + Fun. You see, I believe if you're to enjoy the same success as some dealers I know, you must show people who join your organization an opportunity to grow in their careers. This doesn't necessarily mean everyone can become a manager. It does mean they cannot be allowed to feel they are on a dead-end street, with nowhere to go.

Next, people will run through walls for you and your organization if they feel they can make money. Good money to one can be so-so money for another. Suffice it to say, the people working for you must feel they are being rewarded properly.

Last, people must enjoy their jobs. It's got to be fun to work for you and your company. If I dread going to work every day, how effective will I be? Put some fun in your business. Make people enjoy being there. This feeling usually starts when you're happy and excited to be at work, when you show you are happy and motivated.

Be the obnoxiously happy, smiling person who always says good morning with a giant grin. Look your people in the eye and with a big smile tell them you're happy to see them.

Overcongratulate success and underemphasize people's shortcomings.

CATCH SOMEONE DOING SOMETHING RIGHT, TODAY

Put your performers on a pedestal. Let them bask in the glory. Remember, however, the definition of a performer is one who exceeds the reasonable goals you set for them, not just the top seller in your company.

Set achievable targets for your organization and then cause everyone to celebrate with you when you achieve the goal. Remember, the biggest buildings are built one brick at a time. Post your company's goals where everyone can see them. And, of course, make sure everyone can see they've achieved the goal.

Train all the people in your organization to realize they are in the sales department—everyone is. The person who answers the phone is in the sales department as soon as he or she speaks with a customer or prospect. The person who cleans the building is in the sales department as soon as a customer or prospect walks into your building.

Convince everyone in your organization that no one can make them have a bad day, no one can ruin their attitude. Only they can ruin their own day or attitude by allowing someone else to affect them.

The only downside to all of this is that some of your employees will swear you must be on drugs to be so up all the time. I get accused of this all the time.

A winning, positive, motivated, happy, and enthusiastic environment will produce success 99 percent of the time. Take your chances with the 1 percent.

17

Assemble the Troops—
Sales Meetings Motivate

Sales meetings help you manage and motivate your salespeople. This is true only if you follow some basic rules:

1. Sales meetings should be held at basically the same time every time. If you expect your salespeople to manage their time effectively, they must know what time your meetings will be and how long the meeting will last. Then, they can plan their day around that plan.

2. Sales meetings must always end on time. If your meeting is scheduled to end at 11:00 AM, it must end at 11:00 AM, even if you have to end in the middle of a topic. Stick to the schedule.

3. Attendance must be mandatory. If you make meetings an option, the people who need them most won't attend. If the meetings are structured properly and carefully thought out, everyone benefits. So make attendance mandatory.

4. Everyone must be on time. Stragglers to a meeting are disruptive, often causing you to repeat important things said earlier. Now you're wasting the time of the people who were on time, as well as making it more difficult to stay on schedule and end on time. Consider your meeting an appointment the salespeople have with you. They shouldn't be late for an appointment with a prospect and they shouldn't be late for an appointment with you.

5. No phones, beepers, or PA announcements should be allowed to disturb the meeting. And unless it's an emergency, no interruptions from others in your company.

SALES MEETING OUTLINE

Meetings should be structured as follows: approximately one third information, one third education, and one third motivation, in that order.

Information

If the meetings are to be one hour long, approximately 20 minutes of the meeting will be devoted to gathering and disseminating information. Each person in the sales organization will be asked in front of their peers:

1. How much have you sold since the last meeting? The number given will be compared to the forecast number to be sold he or she projected at the last meeting.
2. How many leads or referrals did you pick up from those sales?
3. How did you get the leads for the sales you made?
4. How much will you sell by the next meeting?

The answers to the questions are posted on a white board in the meeting room. It is hard for a salesperson to attend meeting after meeting and tell you he or she didn't sell anything. It's easier to knock on doors than face the embarrassment. For those who sold, it gives them a chance to be recognized before their peers. They have the opportunity to strut with pride.

If, before the meeting begins, you're aware a salesperson made either a spectacular sale or a sale as a result of prior training from you, you have the opportunity to make a big deal of the salesperson, pumping that individual's ego or, in case of the latter, you're able to reinforce that training is good and smart salespeople succeed when they utilize the training.

Education

Twenty minutes of the meeting will be devoted to education. Now is the time to improve sales skills. This is a perfect time to play a training audiotape, show a portion of the video *Handling Objections and Closing the Sale*, have one of your more successful salespeople address the group on how he or she is able to sell so much, share a successful lead generation method one of your salespeople has discovered, or to spend this time role playing in groups of two.

The sales business is one of constant education. You never know it all. I learn something almost every time I do a seminar. Education is motivational. When salespeople learn more, they sell more and, therefore, they make more money. And making more money rarely demotivates anyone.

Motivation

The final 20 minutes is devoted to motivation—exciting the group, powering them up for the day or week ahead. Never—I repeat, never—end a meeting on a down note. Don't cause your people to leave your meeting depressed. Always end a meeting on a motivational note.

This is a good time to announce a contest. This is a good time to recognize performers. This is a good time to announce the winners of a previous contest. Show a motivational video. Do anything and everything you can to fire them up. They'll run through walls for you if you do this. More important, they will make more sales. And, as little Edith (Lilly Tomlin) used to say, "and that's the truth!"

HOW OFTEN SHOULD I CONDUCT SALES MEETINGS?

Too often, sales meetings are infrequent and disorganized. As a result they are boring, disruptive to the salesperson's schedule, and ineffective.

I prefer daily sales meetings. Daily sales meetings energize the salespeople for the day ahead. It is even harder to stand up in a sales meeting in front of your peers and management every day and say you've sold nothing. You can't procrastinate. You can't put off for tomorrow something you should do today, because tomorrow the manager is going to ask you if you did what you were supposed to do. When the meeting is held weekly, you can procrastinate for at least six days before having to face the manager.

Daily sales meetings help the salesperson remain focused. And if I see a salesperson in trouble, I find out quicker, perhaps in time to intervene and offer help. Some of the most successful sales organizations I work with, selling 1200 plus systems every month, hold daily sales meetings.

$$18$$

Battlefield Incentives—
Sales Contests

While it may seem to some that sales commissions easily should be enough to motivate a sales force, sales contests cause salespeople to achieve above and beyond expectations. Sales contests also can demotivate salespeople if you're not careful.

Mixing up the way one wins a contest keeps it fun and interesting. Design contests in such a way as to recognize achievement and growth versus always honoring the biggest performer. Contests also should be designed to reward a desired behavior. For example, if picking up referrals on sales made is a desired behavior, and of course it is, then design a contest that rewards the salespeople for picking up referrals.

If improving one's closing percentage is a desired goal, then reward that behavior. Design a contest that tracks and rewards the best closer or the most improvement in closing. Since I want all the salespeople in my organization to sell every day and to increase their personal numbers every month, I may want to design a contest that measures personal growth, rewarding the most improvement.

I know and so should you, Saturdays and Sundays are the two best days to make sales. More people are home, with more time on their hands. Good salespeople working on just those two days could out produce equally good salespeople working the five days during the week. Just think what could be produced if your salespeople decided to work Wednesday through Sunday, taking off Monday and Tuesday. Here are some ideas for contests.

REFERRAL POKER

Shuffle two decks of cards together (more if your sales organization is really big). During the contest month, have your salesperson pick a card from the deck, without seeing which card is being picked, for every documented referral turned in with a sale. Someone who picked up three referrals on a sale gets to pick three cards.

Do this all throughout the month or week, for however long you're running the contest. At the end, the salesperson with the best poker hand wins. This contest employs skill, picking up leads, and luck—the luck of the draw—and it can be fun, too.

SALES BINGO

At the beginning of a month, take seven playing cards, ace through seven, and shuffle them. Starting with the first day of the month, pull a card and write down its value on day 1 of a calendar. Let's say the value was three. Pull another card for day 2, let's say it was six. Continue through the seven cards until you marked the first seven days. Reshuffle the cards and start over until you have filled every day of the month with a number.

When you announce the contest, explain that each day of the month has a point value of anywhere between one and seven. The point value already has been placed on a calendar and no one will know how much each day is worth until the end of the contest.

As each sale is brought in during the contest, record the day it was turned in. That's how many points were earned for the sale. The winner is the salesperson who earned the most points by the end of the month.

Once again, both skill and luck are involved. And the mystery adds a bit of excitement.

HIGHEST PERCENTAGE OVER QUOTA

A very basic contest designed to reward personal growth is one that rewards the highest percentage over quota. The hardest part for management is to establish fair and equitable quotas (expectations) for each member of the sales team. Once done, this contest gives everyone, even the newest member of the sales team, a shot at winning. As I said earlier, sometimes sales contests can demotivate people. If only the big gun wins, the remaining salespeople quit on the contest. They don't even try. A contest like this one motivates everyone because anyone can win.

GREATEST CLOSING PERCENTAGE

The key here is the ability to document every presentation. Otherwise, some devious salesperson will conveniently forget a few or more of the sales he or she didn't close to better the closing number. Also, don't accept excuses. A presentation is a presentation.

HIGHEST PERCENTAGE INCREASE IN CLOSINGS

This contest is the same as the one rewarding the greatest closing percentage, only you're rewarding the salesperson whose closing percentage grew the most, not necessarily the best closer.

HIGHEST DOLLAR AVERAGE

This contest rewards a behavior that improves your profitability. It's been documented that generating orders with more dollars per sale both increases profit margin and decreases attrition. Both are good for the company. Rewarding the salesperson whose per sale dollar average is highest is rewarding a behavior that's good for you and the salesperson.

HOW OFTEN SHOULD CONTESTS BE RUN?

Often, is the easy answer—every month. Overlap monthly contests with a quarterly contest. Run a contest over a weekend; for example, on Friday, announce a weekend contest. The salesperson who sells the most units between now and 10 AM Monday morning wins.

Great salespeople are competitive. They love to win. They want the right to claim they're the best. Take advantage of that competitive spirit with sales contests. The prizes they win aren't as important as the prestige winning bestows on them. Give them a chance to take a bow, and they'll reward you with increased sales performance.

WHAT DO THEY WIN?

I just said the prize isn't as important as the recognition, but it still is important. Don't be chintzy. Here are a few examples of rewards for winning:

1. *Cash.* If the winner receives $500 for winning, at the start of the contest, form a $500 bundle of $1 bills. Wrap it in clear plastic and have it with you at the announcement meeting. Show them the money. Throw the

bundle to one of them and have them pass it around the room. (This is why I suggest you wrap it in clear plastic. You want to be sure you get back all $500.)

2. *A Weekend for Two at a Nice, Close Location.* If you choose this one, get brochures of the location before the meeting. Mail brochures to the salespeople's homes, timed to arrive the same day as the meeting or, at worst, the next day. The mailed brochure should include a letter from you announcing the contest and the rules. If they are married, their spouses will get excited too and help motivate the salespeople to win.

3. *Dinner for Two at a Nice Restaurant.*

4. *A Color TV.*

5. *A Nice Suit from a Local Clothier.*

6. *A Month Long Preferred Parking Spot.* Make it close to the entrance to your office, complete with a sign with the winner's name and picture.

7. *Big Wheels.* For a big contest, provide the use of a rented or leased Cadillac for the following month.

Just use your imagination. You'll come up with creative, fun, motivating contests and prizes that will pay dividends to you.

19

Medals of Honor—Awards and Commendations

If you follow a plan similar to the one described in the last chapter and you develop intermediate goals throughout the year, the year will shoot by and before you know it, it'll be year end. Don't miss the opportunity to motivate your people for another year as well as publicly praise the members of your organization who performed well during the year. It's so easy to get wrapped up in the trials and tribulations of the day-to-day business world that we forget or don't make time to recognize the people who have worked hard.

When I operated a successful security alarm and patrol company, we held an annual awards and recognition banquet. At the time, my company was a franchisee of Dictograph Security. Every year Dictograph held a convention at which it recognized the top three salespeople in each division, the top three sales managers, and a variety of other people in various classifications. We enjoyed the conventions and especially enjoyed winning. Dictograph was successful in driving up my company's performance because we wanted to win, we wanted the limelight and recognition of our peers. We took a lesson from Dictograph and developed our own mini awards presentation back home in New Orleans.

We usually rented a nice meeting room at a hotel and had the whole affair catered. It started with an open bar and followed with a nice dinner. After dinner, we began the awards. Like Dictograph, we wrote speeches for every category. My managers and I made the presentations, always keeping the winners secret. The bigger the surprise, the better it was received. Our employees thoroughly enjoyed it, as did we.

We established the following awards:

1. The first-, second-, and third-place sales performer.
2. Rookie salesperson of the year.
3. Most improved salesperson.
4. Team leader of the year.
5. Sales manager of the year.
6. Administrative excellence award.
7. Installer of the year.
8. Service technician of the year.
9. Most improved installer.
10. Most improved technician.
11. Right mental attitude award.
12. Employee of the year.

These awards were presented in an Academy Awards fashion. The recipients were even asked if they wanted to say a few words, and some did.

On a couple of occasions, we seized the opportunity to poke fun, too. One particular year, a customer called a few days after an installation to report a problem. Apparently, after the crew installed the system, a water leak developed, staining a dining room wall. Most often when we received a call like that, on investigating further, the problem turned out to be something we did not cause. So in this case I asked the customer to call a plumber and if the plumber found the problem and any evidence at all indicated the leak was caused by my firm, we would pay for the repairs. The customer agreed.

The next day the customer called back to report the plumber was at her home and the problem without a doubt was caused by the installer. I went to the customer's home to see the evidence.

The plumber traced the problem to a pipe behind the toilet in a second floor bathroom. On opening the wall and exposing the PVC water line feeding the toilet, the cause was clear. An alarm wire was running right through the PVC pipe on its way to the attic. Apparently, when drilling from the window on the first floor, the diversabit used by the installer went up crooked, passing right through the PVC pipe en route to the attic. The installer's helper, waiting in the attic, saw the bit pop through, having no way to know it appeared slightly off track, hooked his wire to it and the installer pulled it down.

We all stood there, staring in amazement at the wire. The plumber couldn't imagine how the installer accomplished the feat. Even the customer saw the humor in the situation. It was an obvious accident, and of course, my company paid for the repair. All I asked in return was the section of PVC pipe removed. On further inspection of the pipe, we noticed that apparently the drill missed going through the first time, making a scar on the side. The second attempt went straight through.

I had the pipe attached to a plaque, with a piece of wire going through the hole and a inscription that said, "If at first you fail, Try, try again!"

We presented it to the installer at the annual awards dinner. Everyone, including the installer, enjoyed a big laugh over the award. However, more important, by giving this award, we said we understand unavoidable accidents do happen, but we still love you.

The annual awards gave us the opportunity to catch our breath once each year and recognize people we should recognize before continuing on to the next year's trials, tribulations, fun, and excitement.

_____ 20

Heal the Sick, Rehabilitate the Wounded, Bury the Dead

Salespeople need help with their careers from time to time. However, remember, salespeople often don't admit needing help. If the problem affecting them doesn't get treated, their careers can suffer, often ending in the demise of a career with your company, in firing.

TYPES OF CONTACT HESITATION

In Chapter 5, we saw how contact hesitation can affect sales performance. The following paragraphs summarize the types of phobias that can attack salespeople.

215

Door Knocking Hesitation

Many veteran salespeople suffer from door knocking hesitation. They know knocking on doors produces results; however, they let one day after another pass without knocking on doors for leads.

Why? Salespeople refuse to knock on doors for numerous reasons. High on the list, is plain old laziness. They just don't want to do it. No hidden and mysterious psychological malady prevents the activity, they just don't want to work that hard. They feel they've grown in sales and shouldn't have to knock on doors anymore. They feel knocking on doors is for the rookies. They perceive it as an unprofessional, entry level only activity.

The problem, of course, is that their sales may suffer as a result. And, while their sales suffer, they can't force themselves to get back out on the street.

Fear of Rejection

Fear of rejection, despite being absent from the psychologist's reasons why salespeople don't make sales contact, is a reality. Some salespeople truly believe today's prospects have matured to the point where direct selling, like knocking on doors, no longer works. People are smarter than that, they proclaim.

Of course, this is just not true. People buy from door-to-door salespeople for the same reasons they've always bought: Because the opportunity to look at what is being offered is easy. All you have to do is let in the salesperson, because salespeople who make their living selling door to door are good at creating interest and overcoming objections and hesitation, and because the prospect believes, at least for the moment, he or she will benefit by owning the product or service the salesperson is selling.

Some salespeople trying to sell at the door are sure the prospect will not be interested in what they are offering for sale. Every rejection further supports their preconceived belief, causing them to project their belief at every subsequent door. The more they knock, the worse they become. It doesn't take much of this punishment to convince a salesperson to forever exclude door-to-door selling from their repertoire.

Making matters worse, whenever you mention door-to-door selling to a nonsalesperson, the reaction you get is negative. They feel door-to-door selling must be cruel and unusual punishment, something they never could do.

With all this negative programming in mind, why is it a surprise salespeople hesitate to add knocking on doors to their repertoire. To go out and knock on doors in the face of all this negativity, to do so with enthusiasm and the belief one needs to truly succeed, is akin to diving from a cliff into a sea of sharks while hundreds of people too terrified to even stand close to the edge look on. Only suicidal people do that.

It's not fun to be rejected time and time again. However, the professional salesperson doesn't feel the same rejection as the weak salesperson. The pro is challenged by the rejection. He or she sees the process as almost a game. A game one can win by shrugging off rejection and moving on to the next door. The pro knows the numbers will work in his or her favor. The pro knows he or she will succeed by pressing on. The pro subscribes to the selling by the numbers philosophy, which suggests you get paid for everything you do. You get paid for the noes equally as well as the yeses.

The pro looks at selling like baseball. The best hitters hit the ball less than one third of the time they come up to bat. They fail two out of three times. However, like the professional salesperson, the professional baseball player understands the numbers game. Ball players know they'll win in spite of the failure that comes along with success.

Empathizer Contact Hesitation

On top of the reasons just mentioned, the psychological fears that restrict one's ability to knock on doors are just as real to the victim and make as much sense to those without the problem as the fear of heights, acrophobia. Fear of heights is illogical. It makes no sense at all. However, when I suffered from acrophobia, I couldn't walk up to an open window and close it if the window was on the second floor of a building or higher. Just as real a fear grips the salesperson suffering from empathizer contact hesitation, when even thinking about knocking on doors.

Telephobia

Telephobia is the fear of prospecting by telephone. Once again, most salespeople would agree that using the telephone to secure more appointments fits in the category of working smarter not harder. They know it can work. However, to some, much like knocking on doors, just the thought of using the phone to make contact with total strangers conjures up deep-rooted fear of rejection.

Weak salespeople rationalize that professionals shouldn't telemarket for leads because the customer has become too sophisticated for that. And they won't respect you as a professional, they assume.

Failure to Network

Academically, networking makes good sense. Obviously, the more who know what one sells the better. However, emotionally, calling on friends or, worse, relatives conjures up fear and hesitation capable of crippling sales careers.

Top sales performers can suffer from one or more of the contact hesitation maladies and not really know it. A salesperson can start his or her sales career already infected by a career-limiting disease or suddenly become infected years into a once successful career.

I suffered from a hesitation to sell to or call on neighbors and friends and didn't know it. I was successful despite the problem, I just didn't sell to my friends. In fact, at the time, most of my friends were unaware of how I made a living. Fortunately for my career, I got over the problem. I was lucky, it went away just as mysteriously as it arrived. I never knew I had a problem. All salespeople aren't so lucky.

Social Self-Conscious Contact Hesitation

The salesperson with social self-conscious contact hesitation has a great deal of difficulty calling on people perceived to be more important than he or she. The individual may tell you he or she can sell anyone, anytime; however, the record will reflect something different.

This salesperson will sell to anyone as long as the person isn't important or socially superior, according to the salesperson's beliefs. In some sales careers this problem can be fatal.

Sales Identity/Role Aversion

Embarrassed to be called a salesperson, this individual has been trying to get out of sales since he or she got in. The person hopes to prove worthy to be promoted to sales manager someday, a job he or she would feel much better about. However, once promoted, because of still suffering from sales role aversion, the manager will likely pass on this extremely contagious belief to new salespeople. Under a role averse manager, the disease spreads at epidemic speed.

Analyzer Contact Hesitation

The salesperson suffering from analyzer contact hesitation over-analyzes every situation. This individual spends too much time preparing for a sales call, too much time preparing professional proposals instead of making sales. The salesperson constantly worries about how prospects will perceive him or her as a professional. This salesperson makes too few sales calls, and his or her career suffers as a result.

Commander Contact Hesitation

Commander salespeople have to be and remain in control. They are very assertive, decisive, and even have a tendency to intimidate. They become impatient with prospects who don't react as they expected. They write off prospects who don't immediately cooperate as stupid people not worthy of their time or product—"screw 'em" is their reaction.

COMBATING CONTACT HESITATION

What do you do when you discover one or more of your salespeople suffers from one or more of these problems? Firing them is the easy way out but not necessarily the smart thing to do. Good salespeople are difficult to find, and most, if not all, problems can be cured.

Work with your salespeople. Make calls with them, as an observer. You can learn a lot about them if you do. If you go on calls with your salespeople, here are some suggestions for getting the maximum results out of the experience.

1. You are there to observe, not to sell for them. You must have the courage to watch the sale go down in flames without butting in. If you jump in to "save" the sale, the salesperson will rarely agree that he or she was going to lose the sale. The salesperson will feel he or she would've sold without you there. So, keep quiet. Let the salesperson lose the sale if that's what is going to happen.

2. Have the salesperson introduce you as an associate, not the boss. If you're introduced as the manager, the prospect will want to do business with you, not your

salesperson; and your reason for tagging along will evaporate right before your eyes.

3. Take mental notes, not written ones. If you want to witness your salesperson's five-day deodorant pad fail in one day, take written notes during the presentation. Even if you are jotting down good things about the individual, he or she will feel that something was wrong.

4. After the sales presentation, arrange to meet with the salesperson at a local coffee shop to talk. Learn and practice the "three pats and a kick" method of critiquing. Salespeople have and need big egos. They must believe in their ability to influence people. The last thing you want to do is deflate your salesperson's ego. (The method is discussed later in this chapter.)

5. Meet with your salespeople regularly. Review their progress toward their personal goals. Get to know their moods and habits. If you do, you'll discover problems much earlier, perhaps in time to help.

6. Test your salespeople with instruments designed to uncover problems when you hire them and then test them once each year thereafter. Early detection can minimize damage.

7. Motivate your salespeople. Most salespeople, and people in general, work harder when inspired to do so.

8. Compensate good performance. If you want great results, pay for performance. Never limit your salesperson's income. Why should you? What does it accomplish?

9. Love your salespeople. They can tell when you don't. I've met all too many sales managers and general managers who depend on the sales made by their salespeople yet hate salespeople. They don't like them, and it shows. If you can't learn to love and respect the abilities of your salespeople, stay far away from them.

Hire someone who can love and respect your salespeople for you.

THREE PATS AND A KICK CRITIQUE STYLE

Brand new salespeople and veterans alike will have moments when they are not performing up to par. Sometimes, they don't know what to do in a given situation. Other times, they forget the skill needed. Still others, especially in the case of the veteran salesperson, consciously choose to eliminate a step in the selling plan for what they believe to be good reasons. Let me give you an actual example.

In the early 1980s, when I was a franchisee for Dictograph Security Systems, I managed and trained a rather large group of salespeople. At the time, we sold systems that averaged in the area of $2500 to $3000 in sales price plus $22 per month. We sold to an upscale client, one who could afford to buy.

Dictograph, through years of trial and error, developed a presentation for salespeople to use on a presentation in the home. Each step of the presentation was designed to take the salesperson closer to the sale. Each step was designed to educate and motivate the prospect to buy. It was a professional presentation that produced results time and time again.

Part of the challenge a salesperson faced in trying to convince the prospect of the need for a professionally installed alarm system was showing them the dangers they faced without an alarm system protecting their home and family. We had to break down their personal psychological law of self-exception, which said they wouldn't have a problem—hadn't had one yet, wouldn't have one in the future. We had to vividly demonstrate how effective an alarm system could be in deterring and stopping a burglary.

To do this, we started by explaining how a burglar selects a home to burglarize. How one might wait outside a home waiting for evidence the resident inside is asleep. The presentation went something like this.

The Sales Pro: Let's suppose, Jack, you are on a business trip, which you've said you go on often enough, and Mary, you're at home with the children. It's 10:00 PM, the children are in bed, and Mary, you're putting the dishes away, ready to go to bed. The whole time a burglar is outside in the dark watching your home, waiting patiently for a sign you've retired for the night.

You know, Jack and Mary, we are all creatures of habit. We tend to do the same things day in and day out. And the burglar knows this. While waiting, he sees the lights go out downstairs. The hall light by the stairs goes on, then off, as you reach upstairs. Your bathroom light goes on, then off, and finally your bedroom lamp will go off. At this point, he feels you've gone to bed. What he doesn't know, Jack and Mary, is that you've done one more thing. You turned on your security system.

Since the burglar has time, he'll probably wait till he feels you are asleep. He might even throw some small pebbles on the roof to see if the sound awakens you, causing you to turn on a light. If nothing happens and a reasonable time has passed, he will proceed to a side or even front door to break in.

It's then when he uses his universal house key to gain entry into your home. Have you ever seen a universal house key?

Jack and Mary (shaking their heads): No.

The Sales Pro (reaching into a briefcase and pulling out a crowbar): Here's one. You see, in the hands of a burglar this is a key. It will open any door. It also is a weapon.

With this crowbar in hand, the burglar approaches a side door. Now you have to know that the burglar's goal is to steal the possessions you own and not wake you. He doesn't know if you have a gun and will use it. He doesn't want to meet you. He'll try to be as quiet as he can be, making little or no noise. He's even careful to not step on twigs for fear the sound of them breaking will waken you.

(The salesperson continuing to describe the break-in lowers his or her voice, speaking softer and softer, causing the prospects to lean forward to hear.) Next the burglar inserts the crowbar between the door and door jamb and applies pressure.

(While explaining, the salesperson uses the crowbar to pry open the door on the demo kit, which already has been armed.) Suddenly the door separates enough from the jamb to allow it to swing open and then . . . (The siren in the demo kit blares out at approximately 90 decibels, startling Jack and Mary.)

The Sales Pro: Mary, I don't want to presume you'd ever be in a situation like this, as the burglar, but if this were to happen to you, what would you have done?

Mary: Why I think I'd have a heart attack! That siren nearly scared me to death!

The Sales Pro (with a big smile): You know, Mary, we often find dead burglars on doorsteps for that very reason. Jack, what would you have done had you been this burglar?

Jack: Why I would run like hell.

The Sales Pro: You know, Jack and Mary, that's most often what happens. The burglar is so startled by the siren and doesn't need or want the attention it is bringing, he most often just runs away. And isn't that what you both want to have happen should a burglar choose your home to burglarize?

Jack and Mary: Yes, of course.

And the salesperson was well on the way to closing the sale.

This presentation was required learning at Dictograph. It was good, it made the point, it was accurate, and it sold systems.

One day I received a call from the manager of one of the offices, who explained that a top producer was in a terrible slump and she was worried about him. She asked if I could call him to see if I could offer some help.

When I spoke with Dave, the salesperson, he explained he hadn't closed a sale in the last 17 presentations. He was depressed, and frankly, he was questioning his career choice.

I asked Dave if he used the presentation he learned years earlier. He said he did. I asked if he changed anything about his work habits. He said no.

I then suggested we role play the last presentation he did, which was the previous evening. He agreed. As I asked what he did first, second, third, and so on, he relived the presentation with me. All the way to the point he said good-bye at the door. No sale number 17.

One thing was missing from his presentation, however. He didn't mention talking about the universal house key. It never came up. I asked Dave about this, to which he explained he didn't use that step any longer. I asked, "Why?"

Dave explained that, some time ago, he did the step exactly as taught and, when he pried open the demo kit door and the siren sounded, he startled the lady so badly she fell back in her chair, clutching her chest. "I thought she was having a heart attack," Dave explained. "I vowed never to do that again."

"Dave," I asked, "did that couple buy the system?" "Yes," he said.

"And did they need the system you sold them?" "Yes," Dave said.

"Did she actually have a heart attack?" I continued. "No," Dave replied, "I thought she was having one."

"Think back, Dave. Did this incident happen approximately 17 no sales ago?"

You see, Dave, the professional salesperson, modified his presentation for the wrong reasons. He strayed from what worked, and his career was paying for it. As managers of salespeople, it's important we know what our successful salespeople do, so we can know what they are doing wrong or different that may explain why they are in a slump.

It's like being Tiger Woods's coach. Tiger, at this time, is the best golfer playing the game. However, even Tiger needs and wants his coach to watch his game closely for fear he will pick up a bad habit that could adversely affect his game and, therefore, his chance of winning and earning a living.

Dave worked in an office hundreds of miles away from mine. If I had the opportunity to spend time with Dave on an appointment I would've noticed his presentation change and would've been in a position to use the three pats and a kick critique style to nudge him back on course. Here's how I would have critiqued Dave using the "three pats and a kick" style.

After losing the sale, I would have suggested we go to a coffee shop or restaurant. At the coffee shop I'd begin the critique.

> Me: Dave, there is no question in my mind, you're a real professional. You are and can continue to be one of our industry's best. (Pat 1)
> In reviewing the appointment we just left, I noticed how professionally you took control from the moment we got there. Your warm-up was great. There is no question Jack and Mary liked you and warmed up to you. (Pat 2)
> And the way you sold Jack and Mary on our company and the services we provide was exceptional. Not only were they impressed with our company, after hearing your presentation of our company, I felt proud to be associated with XYZ, Inc. (Pat 3)
> Dave, how do you feel about the way the appointment went?
> Dave: Well, we didn't get the sale.
> Me: True enough. Can you put your finger on why?
> Dave: No, not really.
> Me: Dave I'm not sure either, you did so many good things in there; however, I did notice you didn't talk about the crowbar. Is there a reason why?

Dave would've told me what he eventually told me by phone. I then could have explained why the step is important to the process and coaxed him back to the fundamentals.

Even the newest and worst salespeople do good things in a presentation. Learn to spot the good qualities and point them out, at least three of them, before you point out the weaker areas. By doing so, you are inflating the person's ego, thus allowing room for a bit of deflation. Also, after receiving praise, salespeople are much more likely to accept and learn from criticism.

Sometimes, salespeople fail because they refuse to do what they should do to succeed. Having little to do with the training you provide, they choose to do or act differently and so do not achieve the success of which they are capable.

For example, when I sold Kirby vacuum cleaners door to door, we were taught a presentation that worked. The presentation was designed to point out all the features the system offered, along with the financial benefits the product accrued to the owner. The financial benefits along with the physical benefits easily justified the investment required to buy a Kirby. If a salesperson took shortcuts in the presentation, some valuable justification was not presented, making the decision to purchase more difficult. The salespeople who refused to use some of the techniques did so because they didn't feel comfortable using them.

For example, one feature the Kirby provided was the ability to extract harmful body ash from a mattress. That part of the presentation began with the salesperson asking the prospect where the dirtiest part of their home was. The answer given by the husband often was the garage. The wife usually said the kitchen or laundry room. At that point the salesperson was supposed to say, "let me show you," walk into the master bedroom, pull back the bedspread and sheet, place the Kirby equipped with a special filter on the bed, and turn it on. All of this was done very quickly, before the prospect had time to object.

As the prospects looked on, the Kirby began sucking up a fine gray powdery substance that could be seen clearly through the glass cover on the attachment where the bag normally would be attached. After a couple of seconds of running, without moving the vacuum, the filter usually was full of the gray body ash.

Next the salesperson would ask if the prospects awoke every morning with a bad taste in their mouths — kind of pasty? "Do you awake with morning breath?" the salesperson would ask.

"Sure," the prospects would answer.

The salesperson then would open a book and read a quote from a Kansas City laboratory stating that humans shed skin. While we sleep, we toss, turn, and roll around in our beds, shedding skin the whole time. This skin grinds into the sheet and the mattress. In fact, the Kansas City laboratory said, after three years of use, you have shed sufficient skin and ground enough of this fine gray skin powder into your mattress to form another person.

"Did you know you were sleeping with another person?" the salesperson would ask. Yuck! This was a chilling thought. The report went on to explain how colds and germs spread through this body ash.

The next question was an easy one. "Jack and Mary, would you invest 25 cents a day to be sure you and your family never have to sleep with this stranger in your bed again?"

When the full presentation was given, the salesperson's chance of getting the sale was far greater. I closed over 50 percent of the presentations I made. However, some salespeople could not or would not ask the "dirtiest part of the home" question along with performing the steps that followed. And, of course, their success was affected.

Remember the "can do, will do" requirement in selling. Learn what your salespeople are doing and, as important, what they are not doing. Their success and yours depends on it.

BURY THE DEAD

What if I do all I should and a salesperson won't or can't follow through? Then, what do I do?

Cut your loses and move on. This is in your best interest and ultimately the salesperson's best interest. Keeping a failing salesperson on staff hurts you, your company, the salesperson, and the successful people on your sales staff. Let me tell you how I learned this valuable lesson.

In 1978, my company was doing well and beginning to grow. As always, I was in need of another good salesperson. At the time, Debbie and I double-dated with close friends of ours, Harry and Peggy. Harry was a successful computer salesperson. He made good money and seemed to love what he did.

Over time, however, I began to notice a problem developing between Harry and his employer. They weren't getting along. Harry was becoming disenchanted with his career. While I wasn't happy Harry's career was suffering, I couldn't help but see an opportunity to inherit a good salesperson.

Conditions finally got to the point that Harry quit his computer job. And, as I hoped, I hired him. However, right from the beginning of Harry's employment with me, I noticed something wrong. Harry wasn't getting into the spirit of the security alarm business. He used computer terminology instead of alarm terminology when he spoke. Unfortunately, Harry was a dismal failure in the alarm business. However, because of our friendship and because I was too weak to do what I should have done, I didn't fire Harry. Harry didn't quit either, perhaps due to his personal friendship with me. The draw against commission I was paying him hurt my company. However, the small amount of money the draw represented to Harry wasn't enough to support him either. We both were miserable.

Finally when the money I was paying without results became too great, I mustered the strength to do what I should have done at least a year earlier. I finally let Harry go.

The interesting thing is what happened next. Harry went back into the computer sales business and became successful again, almost overnight. He was doing what he knew how to do and, I suspect, what he loved to do. He was making a good living again to boot.

Then I realized, once and for all, I was doing Harry no favor by not firing him, nor was I doing any favors to myself and my company either. The best thing I could have done for all concerned was to send Harry on his way toward another career. I should have done so much sooner.

I now believe that I owe it to salespeople I hire to let them go if they're not succeeding in working for me. I owe it to them to convince them to find employment where they can achieve the success everyone deserves. To make that happen I may have to fire the salesperson.

In summary,

1. Hire salespeople you feel stand a chance of being successful. Test them for contact hesitation. If they're too sick at the onset, don't hire them.
2. Test your salespeople once each year to see if they've developed contact hesitation.
3. Thoroughly train the salespeople you hire, providing them with the tools they need to succeed.
4. Develop a planned presentation designed to take the salesperson from "hello" to "thanks for your order."
5. Meet with your salespeople regularly—daily is best, but weekly at worst.
6. Find out what motivates your salespeople to perform. Get their agreement on a proposal to achieve their goals. Have them sign it and then manage them toward their goals.
7. Set expectation of performance for all salespeople. Post results where all can see them.
8. Constantly train your salespeople. The daily sales meeting is an excellent time to do so.
9. Establish regular sales contests designed to reward desired behaviors.
10. Reward performance. Use your champions as an example for others in your organization to follow.

11. Don't allow negativity to exist in your company. When you find it growing, dig it out and discard it as you would a weed strangling the life out of your vegetable garden.
12. Manage your salespeople in the field. Work with them. Learn what they're doing and not doing.
13. If you find problems developing within a salesperson, work with the individual, attempt to rehabilitate him or her.
14. However, if you've tried and nothing seems to work, cut your loses. Send the salesperson to seek another career where he or she stands a chance of succeeding.
15. One last point: Set high standards for achievement in your company. Like water, your people will rise to the standard set. Don't allow mediocrity to exist, not even if the person who isn't achieving is happy. The mediocre salesperson will adversely affect new people you hire, sending confusing signals. When you surround yourself with champions, new people aspire to be champions, too. You've heard the saying "Misery loves company." This is true as well: "Success begets success."

21

A Case Study

As we arrived at Frank Benson's office in Memphis, Frank asked Dorothy, his assistant, "Have you heard from Jamie yet?"

"No, I tried reaching him around 11 last night at the hotel and then again this morning before coming in. No one's seen him. He and his Jackson, Mississippi, salespeople were supposed to arrive last night at around 8 or 9."

"Let me know when you hear from him. I'm a bit worried, after that bad automobile accident he had a couple of months ago. I hope everything's all right."

Jamie Benson, the manager for Frank's Jackson, Mississippi, office is Frank's brother.

A few minutes later the receptionist informs Frank he has a phone call on line 2.

"I can step into the lobby if you need some privacy," I suggest.

"That's OK, Lou, just sit there."

"Hello this is Frank Jr.," he says to the caller.

Frank Benson Sr., Frank's father, works with him in the business. They've almost always worked together, and so Frank

Jr. has become accustomed to referring to himself as Junior. All of his friends just call him Junior, and that pretty much means everyone Frank knows. Frank Jr. has never met a stranger. He appears to like everyone, and everyone appears to like him. Frank's quick, somewhat impish, smile brings a smile to the face of people in his presence. You have to like him, you can't help it, a fact, I suspect, that has helped him immensely in sales.

> Connie: Frank, this is Connie Watson with Triple A Security, we're an authorized dealer also. We met in Florida last month at the dealers meeting.
>
> Frank (lying): Sure Connie, I remember meeting you. What can I do for you?
>
> Connie: Frank, everyone knows you've been successful in this alarm dealer program, selling almost 1000 systems a month. Is that right?
>
> Frank (proudly): We'll sell over 1200 this month.
>
> Connie: Wow! I've got to learn the secret, which is why I'm calling. At the dealer meeting you said you wouldn't mind answering a few questions, would right now be OK?
>
> Frank (smiling, hardly a week goes by he doesn't receive a call or two from another dealer wanting to learn the secret to his success): Sure, Connie, fire away.
>
> Connie: How does your organization get the majority of its sales. How do you locate prospects to sell to?
>
> Frank: Connie, most of our sales comes by way of good old-fashion feet on the street door knocking. We see the people.
>
> Connie: Door knocking, huh?
>
> Frank: Yea, door knocking.
>
> Connie: What times of day do you knock on doors, Frank?
>
> Frank: Well, we start every day around 9 AM, after the sales meeting.
>
> Connie: When do you stop?
>
> Frank: After the porch lights go out.

Connie: Oh, well, anyone could be successful working that hard.

Frank: That's true, anything else?

Connie: No, that'll do it for now. Thanks.

Frank: No problem, good-bye.

Smiling again, Frank looks at me and says, "I'm always getting calls like this. They want to know the big secret. Hell, there is no big secret. It all depends on the whether, Lou—whether or not they are willing to work hard. That's the secret, plain and simple. Hard work.

"They have to be willing to do what it takes. Start early, finish late. Drive to any neighborhood, get out of the car, and start knocking on doors—not some doors, all doors. If they do that every day, all day, they'll make sales. Period. They'll find people at home who will spend a few minutes listening to what they have to offer. And a lot of those people will feel the need and buy. It's just that simple, isn't it, Lou? Or am I just crazy."

"You're not crazy," I answer. "You're the proof it works. See the people. Too many salespeople want a shortcut to success. My experience tells me that shortcuts usually result in short success and short money. A shortage of everything needed."

Just then Dorothy walks in the office. "You told me to let you know when I heard from Jamie, here he is."

Jamie Benson walks in with a big smile and an enthusiastic "Good morning!" Jamie extends his hand, "Hi, Lou."

"Good morning," I reply.

"What happened to you, Jamie." Frank asks. "We were all worried when you didn't check into the hotel last night."

"What's the fuss, Junior? It's a fairly long drive from Jackson to Memphis and we got bored along the way. We were passing so many nice neighborhoods, we decided to stop at a few along the way and knock on doors. Hell, we sold 11 systems doing that. I've got the contracts and checks right here in my hand."

Frank smiles and holds his right hand high for Jamie's "high five." "You see, Lou, just as I said, hard work!"

"Hell, and it's fun, too," Jamie chimes in. "It's fun!"

As we walk out of Frank's office into the reception area, salesperson after salesperson walks in to turn over the paperwork for sales made the day before. There is excitement in the air. High fives are seen everywhere. Frank Jr., in his usual style, greets everyone warmly. Frank loves his people and they love him. You can tell.

"Where's the meeting gonna be?" one of the salespeople asks.

"Lou is scheduled to do it at the Mt. Moriah Holiday Inn down the street at 9 this morning, don't be late!" he replies.

As we drive to the meeting, I can't help thinking how fortunate I am, how much of a pleasure it is to work with excited, motivated dealers like Frank. How easy my job can be when speaking to an audience like Frank's salespeople. It is kind of like being a preacher preaching to the choir. No problem getting an "Amen" out of them, no problem at all.

Printed in the United States
150814LV00002B/46/A